Joel's Oregon Summer

EDNA MAY OLSEN

Pacific Press Publishing Association
Boise, Idaho
Montemorelos, Nuevo Leon, Mexico
Oshawa, Ontario, Canada

Edited by Marvin Moore
Designed by Tim Larson
Cover Illustration by Lars Justinen
Type set in 11/13 Century Schoolbook

Library of Congress Cataloging in Publication Data

Olsen, Edna May, 1926-
  Joel's Oregon summer.

  Summary: Introduces the plants, animals, and natural beauty
provided by God for the Siuslaw National Forest in Oregon,
through the experiences of a Christian family spending a summer
at a campground there.
  1. Siuslaw National Forest (Or.)—Juvenile literature. 2. Natural
history—Oregon—Siuslaw National Forest—Juvenile literature.
[1. Siuslaw National Forest (Or.) 2. Natural history—Oregon—
Siuslaw National Forest. 3. National parks and reserves. 4. Christian life] I. Title.
F882.S58047   1986   979.5'31   86-20456
ISBN 0-8163-0676-1

86 87 88 89 90 • 5 4 3 2 1

To all children who love the out-of-doors,
this book is dedicated.

Contents

Chapter 1

Discovering Whispering Spruce Campground

The more miles Joel and his parents put between them and the city the higher their spirits rose. It had been a busy year, but now they were free at last to take a long-awaited trip with their trailer for a few weeks of sightseeing and relaxation along the Oregon coast. Joel had brought along several books to read and a thousand other items essential to a twelve-year-old on vacation.

Soon they turned off the freeway and took the winding road along the river to the ocean, heading for Whispering Spruce Campground, which is part of the Siuslaw National Forest. Heavily laden logging trucks lumbered up and down the road, scattering wood chips and bark in all directions. Sometimes they passed peaceful farms with sloping sunlit meadows where contented cattle grazed. In other places trees crowded the highway, making it dark and cool.

Wild irises, buttercups, and foxgloves covered the banks, and little streams trickled gently down the rocky surface of the cliffs on one side of the road.

On the other side ran a wide, gray river on which little fishing boats bobbed and maneuvered as their occupants sought the best fishing areas. Along its muddy banks people searched for crabs and crayfish.

Presently they reached a small town bustling with activity and continued on until they reached Whispering Spruce Campground. Dad pulled up to the entrance behind a big, shiny motor home and shut down the engine.

"Looks like we'll have to wait a bit," he said, relaxing back in his seat. "I do hope they aren't full-up."

"I hope so too," Mom said. "It looks like a lovely place, doesn't it?"

"Wonderful!" Dad replied. "Such huge trees and masses of flowers, and the ocean just a short distance away! I'm sure I could stay here forever."

"We have a much more wonderful home for our 'forever,' " Mom said with a smile, "but I know what you mean. How long do you think we should stay here?"

"How about a week at first," Dad said. "If we like it we can extend. What do you think, Joel?"

"Sounds good to me," Joel replied. "I just can't wait to explore it."

The driver of the motor home was complaining to the ranger. "It's expensive," he said. No electricity and you want five dollars a night! We want to watch the Dodger game tomorrow, and we've *got* to have electricity. He paused and shook his head. "Well, I guess we'll head down the road a bit and check out a few other places. He got back in his motor home, made a U-turn, and sped out of the campground.

Dad got out of the car. "Want to come along, Joel?" he asked. Together they walked over to the ticket booth.

"We'd like a campsite," Dad told the ranger. "For a week at first, then maybe longer. Are there any restrictions on length of stay?"

"The rule is ten days," the ranger said, "but if people cooperate, we can always bend the rules. Here's your envelope. Go ahead and pick your site. "There are lots to choose from. When you've found the one you want, put your money in the envelope and drop it in the box." He pointed to a wooden box beside the ticket booth. "Then put the stub in the window of your vehicle where we can see it when we make our rounds first thing in the morning."

"Do *any* of the sites come with electricity?" Dad asked.

"Only the host site," the ranger said. "And speaking of the host, we don't have one this year. Too bad, because they relieve us of a lot of routine work around the campground. If you've any questions come and see me."

"I have one," Dad said smiling. "Just what is a host?"

"A host is a volunteer who welcomes people to the campground and helps them find a suitable campsite if necessary. He is here to answer questions such as which berries are edible, what trees are in the campground, where to catch fish—that sort of thing. Sometimes he'll check the paper supply in the restrooms or pick up litter, but generally we leave things up to his particular preferences. Most of all, we want the host to boost the national forest and act as a PR person. It's a terrific job for retired people or for someone who has the entire summer off."

Joel had been listening to the conversation with interest. "What does PR stand for?" he asked.

"Public Relations," the ranger explained. "The host is a visible representative of the Forest Service. "The public likes to know someone is there to whom they can turn in case they have a problem, and the rangers can't always be around. It's a great way to meet all sorts of fascinating people, and the actual work involved is quite small."

"I'm a teacher," Dad said slowly. "I have the entire summer free. I think we'd enjoy hosting in a beautiful park like this. Where would I apply to be a host?"

The ranger grinned. "I believe you'd make a great host," he said quickly. "Tell you what. My partner will be here shortly, and I'll discuss it with him. I'm sure he'll need to ask you a few questions, and you'll probably have some yourself. Find a campsite and get set up; then sometime tomorrow morning we'll come over and discuss it with you. In the meantime, you and your family give the matter a little thought."

"Thanks a lot," Dad said. "It sounds very interesting." Then he stuck out his hand. "My name is Rogers. Kermit Rogers."

"Wayne Anderson," the ranger said, and the two men shook hands.

Dad told Mom about the hosting position as they drove slowly through the campground. "There's no pay, of course, but the host site has full hookups, and they won't charge us any fee. What do you think?"

"It sounds great," she said slowly, "but are you sure you want to stay here the entire summer?"

"I can't think of a more pleasant place, can you?" Dad asked. "We decided before we left not to make any firm plans. All we wanted to do was get away from work for a few weeks. The ranger said there wasn't much work involved—mostly meeting people, answering their questions, and keeping the place tidy. We'd have to check the restrooms periodically to make sure they don't run out of supplies, that sort of thing. And once a day we'd go through the camping area and record the license numbers of the vehicles so the ranger can reconcile the records with the money deposited in the box at the gate. We wouldn't handle the money at all, and of course all the park maintenance is done by the rangers."

"It sounds super," Joel said. "I'd rather stay here the entire summer than drive to different places. And I'd be able to help you too. Please tell him Yes, Dad," he pleaded.

"It does make a lot of sense," Dad said. "If you both agree, I'll tell them we'd like the job."

"I'm really excited about it," Mom said happily, "and now let's find a campsite so I can get lunch on the table."

"How about this one?" Dad said, pulling into a site tucked away at the end of a narrow road, almost hidden by tall spruce trees.

"Perfect," Mom said, taking a deep breath of piney air. "There's plenty of shade and lots of sunshine too. And listen!" She paused. "There's a stream over there to lull us to sleep."

"I'm going to explore," Joel shouted, leaping out of the car as soon as Dad had pulled to a stop. "I bet there are fish in the stream, Dad. Come and have a look."

"Later," his father said. "First we've got to get set up. Then it'll be lunchtime, so don't be gone too long."

Joel scrambled along the bank, following the little stream as far as he could, until a tangle of brambles barred his way. He pulled a long, slender willow branch out of the underbrush and trailed it through the water, surprising a shoal of miniature fish that darted out of reach. He crossed the stream, jumping from one stone to another. A green wart-covered toad leaped from under a boulder and hid in the tall reeds on the opposite bank, while overhead a big black crow chattered angrily.

At last, hearing his mother call, he turned reluctantly from the little stream and ambled back to the trailer, where Mom had spread out a tempting lunch on the picnic table.

"What a lovely place," Joel sighed. He turned to his father. "Dad, may I take the inner tube to the stream later on?"

"Of course," his father said, "but hurry and wash your hands. I'm starving."

"Me too," Joel exclaimed eyeing the potato salad and baked beans. "Hold on, I'll be right back."

When Joel returned, Dad gave thanks for their safe journey and for the beauty of God's creation, and he asked for guidance about the hosting job.

"I picked up a brochure from the ranger," Dad said a little later. "There's lots to see and do around here. There are several trails to take, some difficult and some easy, and there's a little tunnel that runs under Highway 101 to the beach and the tide pools. I think if we plan to stay here any length of time we'll try to do them all. That way if we're asked about them we can answer intelligently."

As they ate, the bright black eyes of an inquisitive blue jay stared down at them from a nearby alder. It chattered a minute or two, then grew bolder, and finally, with a shriek of triumph, fluttered down to the ground beside them.

"What a beautiful bird!" Joel exclaimed. "And it is not afraid of us." He dropped a few crumbs on the ground, and the jay gobbled them immediately. "Wow, it must be hungry! See how quickly it ate them."

Mom smiled. "I doubt it's hungry," she said. "It's just greedy, that's all. Human food really isn't good for birds, you know. They should be eating berries and insects."

The blue jay turned its head in all directions looking for more crumbs, then flew back to its perch on the alder.

"I know!" Joel said, jumping up from the table. "I'll get some cracked wheat for it. That shouldn't hurt it, should it?" He dashed into the trailer and returned moments later with a handful of cracked wheat that he sprinkled on the ground beside the picnic table. There was a brilliant flash of blue, and seconds later the jay lighted on the ground and gobbled up every grain. Then, with a shake of its black crest, it spread its wings and flew into the forest.

"It has probably gone to get the rest of its family," Dad chucked. "It knows that we'll feed them!"

A yellow-and-white butterfly lighted on a yarrow flower nearby. Everyone sat quietly admiring it.

"Why are they called 'butterflies'?" Joel asked after the butterfly flew away. "They aren't butter, and they aren't flies."

"When I was a little girl, my grandmother told me they were originally called 'flutterbys,'" Mom said, "but the syllables got reversed over the years.

"Chickadee-dee-dee." The cry of a tiny gray bird came from the forest. "Chickadee." Dad answered the call, softly repeating "chickadee." A minute or two later a chickadee flew to one of the lower branches of the alder tree and watched them curiously.

"Sit perfectly still and speak to him softly," Dad said. "Maybe he'll come to us." But the little gray bird wouldn't come any closer, and finally it flew back into the trees.

When lunch was over and the table cleared, Mom suggested that they take one of the marked trails to the ocean tidepools about two miles away. Leaving the camping area they crossed a small wooden bridge. The stream gurgled and splashed over the stones on its way to the sea. They took a little path into the forest. At times they were forced to walk single file in order to avoid the thorns on the blackberry vines and overgrown salal shrubs.

Presently they came to a giant spruce which, despite the fact that it had lost its top when hit by lightning years ago, still stood taller than any other tree in the forest. From here the path took a sharp upward turn.

The trail was still spongy from recent rains, and in places much of the soil had washed into the stream, making it difficult to proceed. The path led across another bridge, wound up for several yards, and finally led to a moss-covered bench at the very top.

"Let's rest here for a while," Dad panted as he slumped on the bench. Joel, impatient to see what lay ahead, wandered on. Presently he came to the concrete remains of a Civilian Conservation Corps camp. Before the second world war it had been home to hundreds of young men engaged in forestry projects—the building of bridges, recreational facilities, and Whispering Spruce Campground.

Suddenly Joel stopped and stared at the ground. Then he whirled and ran back toward his parents.

"Dad, come and look," he shouted. "There are bear tracks up here!"

Mom shivered. "A bear!" she said. "Are you sure?" She looked through the trees, half expecting one of them to make its appearance.

"It's quite possible," Dad said, getting up from the bench. "But bears won't harm you unless, of course, you should happen to back one in a corner or come between a mother and her cubs. As a matter of fact, they're more afraid of us than we are of them."

Mom looked skeptical, but she walked on up the trail to see for herself.

"Look at those prints!" Joel said, pointing to the tracks in the mud. "He must be huge!" He placed his hand in one of the tracks. It was twice the size of his hand.

"He probably came down the bank to the stream for a drink," Dad said. "I imagine this stream is a very busy place at night." Joel and his parents examined the bear tracks a few more minutes, then hiked on. After another bend or two down the trail they came to a miniature waterfall that trickled down the rocky cliff and joined the stream below. Joel discovered a dozen or more deer tracks, and nearby the tracks of a much smaller animal.

"These are coon tracks," Dad said. "A raccoon only gets to be about three feet long, and a third of that is tail. They like to come around in the evenings for handouts. We'll probably see some of them at the campground."

"I hope we do see some of them," Joel said. "I'll give them something to eat."

Dad explained that it isn't a good idea to let them eat directly from your hand because even though they have good eyesight, they are very eager and have been known to bite off more than the food!

"Is it true, Dad, that raccoons wash their food?" Joel asked.

"Raccoons are very fastidious about their food," Dad replied. "They wash everything before eating it. Of course, sometimes the water isn't as clean as it should be, but at least the animals have good habits."

They continued their walk, stopping every now and then to listen to the call of a thrush or to examine the wildflowers and ferns along the way.

A quarter of a mile down the trail they met a sun-burned young woman swinging a machete who told them she was a school teacher who spent her summers doing volunteer work for the national forest. "They've got me clearing trails," she said. "It's hard work, but I enjoy it." She paused and smiled at Joel. "At first my muscles gave me a bit of trouble, but now that I'm used to it, I feel great. After an hour or two in the forest my frustrations melt away, and I feel renewed in both body and spirit."

She picked up a long section of blackberry bush and threw it over the bank. "My friends think I'm crazy," she giggled, "but I love what I'm doing. Some of them are in Europe, and they'll probably come back more tired than when they went. The crowded airports and stifling cities aren't for me. I love the forest with its towering trees and little damp trails. And, of course, there's the beach. That's fantastic!"

Mom asked if she was camped in the forest, and she said she had a tent in Whispering Spruce Campground. "Stop by some evening for a visit," she said. "There's just me and my old dog, Higgins. He loves it here too."

Joel and his parents said Goodbye and continued on down the trail. They topped a gentle rise, and suddenly the Pacific Ocean lay before them, gray and shining. Countless little fishing vessels sailed near its shore, while on the horizon a freighter carried its cargo to a port farther up the coast.

"Let's go to the beach," Joel said as he ran down the path and through a tunnel under the highway where the trail ended. They scrambled up the bank on the other side of the road and were finally on the beach.

The wind blew fresh and strong, and they trudged across the sand until they reached a group of rocks, across which lay hundreds of logs that had been bleached by the sea and the sun. They picked their way around and over the logs and past huge tangles of sea-weed and rolls of beach grass that the waves had rolled into solid lumps. They stopped occasionally to explore the little tidal pools that teemed with life: hermit crabs camouflaged with scraps of seaweed, starfish searching for clams and mussels, barnacles, and sea anemones.

Finally they sat down on the sand and watched the seagulls as they screamed and quarreled, wheeled and dived in an endless search for food.

"Just look at them!" Mom said. "Watch how they glide and catch the air currents. Wouldn't it be wonderful to be a gull for just an hour?"

Dad chuckled. "Gulls are called the freebooters of the world, you know. They'll steal anything, even taking the eggs and babies out of the nests of the cormorant and other sea birds. Once I saw a gull snatch a fish from a pelican's pouch. And they'll eat all kinds of garbage, like the refuse thrown overboard from ships and anything they can scavenge along the beaches. That's where the word *gullible* comes from. They'll swallow anything."

They watched a passing gull drop a clam on the rocks below in an effort to break the shell. It kept retrieving the shell and dropping it till it was finally broken into pieces, but before the gull was able to enjoy its hard-earned meal a swifter gull seized the meat and flew off with it, leaving the first gull screaming and zooming off in hot pursuit.

"I've heard that the seagull is so much at home in the air it can actually scratch its head while flying," Dad said. "Gulls have been clocked as fast as fifty miles an hour. They can also soar for hours on rising air currents."

"Well," Mom said at last, "I suppose it's time to be heading home." They scrambled to their feet, shook the sand off their clothes, and found the little trail again. They walked back through the damp forest, faster this time, over the little bridges, past the pile of brambles the young woman had chopped, until they reached the campground.

While Mom fixed supper, Joel and his father gathered twigs and pieces of dead wood. Soon a bright fire was sending tiny sparks flying into the darkening sky. A breeze cooled the air, and somewhere in the forest an owl hooted.

"It's lovely here, Dad," Joel said later that evening as he skewered a marshmallow onto a coat hanger. "I hope you can be a host for a couple of months."

"Even if it means working for part of your summer vacation?" Dad asked, and Joel said he wouldn't mind a bit. He thought it would be fun.

The darkness deepened. The forest grew black and still, and the fire burned down until there was nothing left but ashes. The sky was full of stars. When Joel yawned Mom suggested that it was considerably past his bedtime. "And ours too," she added. "It has been a long day."

"Have you made up your mind about the hosting job?" Joel asked at breakfast the next morning. "What are you going to tell the rangers when they come around?"

"What would you like me to tell them?" Dad asked with a twinkle in his eye.

"That you'll be the host here this summer. I can't think of anything I'd rather do than stay here. Please, Dad, say we can."

"Then it's decided," Dad said. "I'll tell them we're all agreed. It'll be a terrific educational experience for all of us, but of course, if we're to answer questions about the area and the names of the birds and flowers, we must learn all we can. We'll go into the library this afternoon and look for some books. I'm sure the ranger has some we can borrow too."

The rangers came by soon after breakfast and asked if they'd thought any more about being hosts for June and July at Whispering Spruce Campground. Dad told them they'd discussed it and decided it was something they'd really enjoy, and the rangers gave him an application form to fill out.

"It's just a formality," the ranger explained. "Although if you should have an accident, the insurance company would need proof that you were employed by us."

One of the rangers went back to the truck and returned with a dark green forest jacket for each of them. Each jacket had a badge on the arm. The rangers also handed Dad the keys to the supply room, a clipboard, and a large box of maps and brochures. "You'll want to study up on these," he said. "You'll be asked all kinds of questions about the area."

"And this," he said, handing Joel a long stick with a nail in the bottom, "is your badge of office. Discharge your duties faithfully."

Joel slipped into his forest jacket and went outside with his stick. He felt very important as he snagged pieces of litter and deposited them in the garbage cans. Now he was part of the National Forest Service, helping to keep the campground clean.

"By the way," one of the rangers said just before they left, "we're having a slide show for all our volunteers over at the visitor center this afternoon—sort of a get-acquainted time. There'll be cookies and punch, too, so you'll enjoy it, I'm sure."

Dad promised they'd be there.

"Then you're on your own," the rangers said. "Good luck."

As soon as they'd gone, Dad towed the trailer over to the host site at the entrance to the campground, where the Stars and Stripes waved, and set it up. Then he pulled out the awnings and placed the deck chairs under the trees.

"Well, what do you think of your home for the next two months?" he asked Joel when he came back. "Not bad, is it?"

"It's great, Dad," Joel said. "And now what are we supposed to do?"

"Nothing much at present," his father said. "Of course, people will be stopping by to ask questions, and we'll help them all we can. For now we might as well walk around the campground and get to know it. We can check the restrooms while we're at it."

"There aren't many people camping here, are there?" Joel said. Dad told him that the rangers had said that in a few days the campground would probably be full. "Enjoy it while you can," Dad chuckled. "Apparently it gets very busy later on."

When they got back to the trailer a Mr. Jenkins from the Department of Agriculture stopped by to see them and left a leaflet for them to read. Then he suspended a little triangular box from a branch of an alder tree nearby. Joel asked what it was for.

"It's a gypsy moth trap," Mr. Jenkins said. "It has been coated with a special scent to attract the male gypsy moth. It's also sticky so that when the moth gets inside it can't get out. I'll be around periodically to check it, and if I find a gypsy moth in the trap we'll have to spray the campground."

"Why?" Joel asked.

"Gypsy moths are very destructive," Mr. Jenkins explained. "They can wipe out entire orchards and forests in a very short time unless they're eradicated. They're terrible pests. Right now they've been found in California and on the East Coast, but none in Oregon so far, and that's the way we want to keep it."

"How did they come to be in this country?" Joel asked.

"It's a strange story," Mr. Jenkins replied. He explained that in 1868 a Harvard astronomer began experimenting with the crossbreeding of silk worms in his spare time, and he brought the gypsy moth to Medford, Massachusetts, by importing eggs from Europe. It was never any trouble in Europe because its numbers had been controlled by birds and other insects, but it liked the conditions it found in America and set out to take possession of the land. Trees in Massachusetts were completely defoliated. Ravenous caterpillars soon covered the sidewalks and houses. Real estate prices plummeted, and people left the area, unable to cope with the problem. The government appropriated hundreds of thousands of dollars to eradicate the gypsy moth, and by 1900 the victory was almost won. In fact, the government was so sure it had gotten rid of the pests that it cut off the money, and in the next five years the area of infestation grew from 359 square miles to 2,224 square miles!

"Since the female cannot fly," Mr. Jenkins continued, "the spread of the gypsy moth depends on free transportation. It attaches itself to cars and is carried to all parts of the United States, where it drops off and breeds new generations. We're particularly concerned with checking campgrounds because people come in from every state, often bringing the pest with them."

"What do they look like?" Joel asked, fascinated by the story.

"They're quite beautiful, I suppose," Mr. Jenkins said. "They're white with bold bands of black. I hope you never see one here though," he said grimly.

Joel checked the little trap almost daily, but fortunately it was always empty.

Chapter 2
Sea Lions
on the Shore

The visitor center was a large circular building with a magnificent view of the Pacific Ocean. Over its wooden deck a delicately carved whale and its baby floated ethereally. Inside were more carvings, displays of fossils, shells, starfish, and other creatures of the sea. On the walls hung photographs of the ocean, early logging days, and pioneer trails long since abandoned to the forest. They recorded the history of Oregon when timber and fishing were thriving industries. They told of great forest fires and destructive gales and of the disappearance of many sea and land creatures at the hand of man.

Joel and his parents went to the visitor center that afternoon where they met other volunteers. Some chopped trails. Others led hikes through the forest and tidepools or conducted slide shows at the campground in the evening. Later they attended a lecture and slide show about whales, although Mr. Dalton, the naturalist, briefly mentioned other sea mammals such as the otter, seal, walrus, and porpoise. "There are many varieties of whales," he said: "The blue, finback, sei, humpback, gray, right, and sperm." Joel had no idea there were so many kinds, and each with its own distinctive blowing and diving characteristics.

Mr. Dalton suggested that they watch for whales in the early morning hours before the wind created whitecaps on the water's surface. "Overcast days are best for whale watching because there is little glare," he said. "Whales have periodic blow patterns during migration and sometimes will make up to half a dozen short, shallow dives before a longer dive of up to ten minutes." He explained that usually a small part of the whale's head and back shows during a "blow." One can tell which variety of whale it is by the shape of the dorsal fin, head, and tail.

" 'Spy-hopping' is a term applied to a whale when its head is partly out of the water and its eyes are above the surface, when," Mr. Dalton said, "the whale takes a look around to see if there are any boats in the vicinity. 'Breaching' describes when the whale rises vertically out of the water, often to half its length, and then falls back on its side or back, making a spectacular splash as it hits the water." He explained that whales do this when courting, communicating with each other, or just having fun. Often, when one whale breaches, the others will follow him as if they were playing follow the leader.

Mr. Dalton explained that as most whales swim through the oceans, they catch small fish and other sea creatures in a bony sievelike structure in their mouths, called baleen. "So it's obvious," he chuckled, "that Jonah was never swallowed by a whale. And, of course, we know that billions of years ago the whale was a land creature, but through evolution adapted itself to the ocean."

Mom put up her hand. "As one who believes in Creation," she began, "I must challenge your last statement, because the book of Genesis says that 'God created great whales.' And," she chuckled, "I can't imagine a whale roaming about on land with his mouth open catching flies and mosquitos; he could never have caught enough to keep himself alive!"

"And," Joel added, "it says that God *prepared* a great fish to swallow Jonah, so it probably wasn't an ordinary whale that swallowed him. It was one God made specially."

"Good for you," whispered the man behind him. "Glad to hear a young man stick up for his beliefs."

"Nevertheless," Mom said later that evening, "it was an extremely interesting lecture. I learned a lot. It made whales 'come alive' for me."

Because of what he had learned at the whale program, each time Joel went down to the ocean after that, he saw more than a vast expanse of empty water. His imagination pictured great whales calling each other in a mysterious language that only they understand. He envisioned mother whales migrating with their young, teaching them to survive in a hostile world where even man seeks to destroy for his own selfish purposes. The walrus that he saw fishing from distant ice floes were real, as were the porpoises frolicking in the sunshine among vast coral reefs and waving seaweed and millions of marvelously colored fish of all shapes and sizes. "There is more life on earth than we see," he mused. "There is the life of the heavens and the life of the ocean as well."

The next day they told the ranger how much they had enjoyed the lecture on whales. "Be sure to visit the sea lion caves down the coast," he said. That afternoon, with binoculars, a camera, and sweaters they set off to see the only mainland home of the wild sea lions.

A steep walkway with incredible views of the Oregon coastline led to the elevator which descended to one of the largest sea caves in the world: 300 feet across—the length of a football field—with a vaulted dome twelve stories high. The only light in this enormous cavern came from the opening covered with steel mesh, beyond which the sea lions battled and roared.

The volcanic, lichen-covered walls were clammy and cold nesting places for the pigeon guillemot. Dad explained that these black-bodied birds with white wing patches don't make nests but lay their eggs directly on the ground. "Some eggs are pearly white, others, cinnamon," he said. "Some are streaked or splotched with black, green, and brown blotches or squiggles, and no two are ever alike. Even among the thousands of eggs on the cliffs each bird knows exactly which is its egg."

"Well, I should think so!" Mom said. "She'd be a poor mother that didn't know her own offspring."

Joel noticed that the guillemot is an awkward creature on land, but in the air the birds rode the currents with ease. Suddenly one dived straight into the ocean. "Dad, did you see that bird!" Joel exclaimed.

His father smiled. "That's how they catch their food," he said. "They swim to the bottom, and, steering with their feet and propelling themselves along with outstretched wings, they feed on shells and small fish."

Mom shivered. "I'm cold," she said. "I move that we go back into the sunshine." They rode the elevator back to the top and looked over the edge of the cliff. Far below on a large rock a short distance off shore a large male seal battled to retain dominance of his herd, fighting off the young bachelor seals that tried to usurp his position as leader. "As time goes by the older seals become weaker with age," Dad said. "At the same time the bachelors are growing stronger, and eventually the positions are reversed. So the cycle goes on."

"Now I know why they're called 'sea lions,'" Joel said. "Listen to their roaring!"

They watched the playful pups crawl over their

sleeping parents, while their yearling brothers and sisters dove into the foaming sea and swam with powerful, leisurely strokes almost like birds in flight. Others fished for skate, squid, or rock fish.

A little farther down the coast, on rocks plastered white with guano, sat a group of cormorants—large, long-necked black birds with yellow faces. "Cormorants enter the ocean head first without the slightest splash and swim with extraordinary speed to capture fish," Dad said. "After a few seconds they bring a fish to the surface, toss it in the air, and let it slide down their long throats, head first. Later they sit on the rocks and let the sun dry their plumage." He went on to explain that the cormorant, noted for its extremely messy nest of sticks and roots lined with seaweed and other shoreline debris, is the famed fishing bird of Japan. The Japanese place it on a leash with a ring around its neck and discipline it to bring its catch to its trainer.

Before returning home Joel and his parents went down to the water's edge. They scrambled over rocks slippery with green slime and coated with barnacles, and they explored the many little tidepools among the rocks where sea anemones wait to catch unwary creatures in their traps. Here and there restless little hermit crabs scampered about, cleaning up dead and dying organisms, using empty snail shells as protection for their soft bodies. They saw brightly painted starfish—purple, orange, and chocolate brown—sticking to the rocks with their tube feet. Joel didn't take any of the sea creatures because he knew that away from their natural habitat they would quickly die.

While they were walking along the beach they met a man searching for agates, a very hard stone with patches or bands of color that is plentiful along the coastline of the Pacific Northwest. Joel asked the man what they looked like.

"That's hard to say," the man replied. "There are tiny clear agates the size of peas that are called teardrops. Others, usually red, brown, or gray, sometimes measure two or more feet in diameter. After they're given a polish, they can be made into beautiful ornaments and jewelry." The man also explained that chalcedony is one kind of agate.

"Oh, that's a Bible word," Mom said. "Revelation 21 describes the Holy City coming down out of heaven from God, and one of the stones in its foundation is chalcedony."

The air was beginning to turn chilly, so Joel and his parents headed back toward their car. Joel kept his eyes on the beach but was unable to find any agates. Though he searched for them often in the days ahead, he never found even one.

Chapter 3
The Spirit of the Forest

"What a wonderful day!" Dad said the next morning as he emerged from the trailer. Mom was hanging out the wash on a line strung between two pine trees. "Who feels like a good long climb up to Orcas Lookout?" Dad asked.

"I do," Joel shouted, throwing down his book. "But isn't that a long way to climb?"

"A little over 800 feet above sea level," his father said. "That's not too strenuous if we take our time, and the view should make it worthwhile."

Mom said she preferred to stay home and write letters and keep an eye on the wash. "Those mischievous blue jays are threatening to ruin my morning's work!" she said.

Joel filled a water flask. Then he and his father waved goodbye to Mom and followed the signposts that pointed to the trail that led to the ridge at Orcas Lookout. At first the trail was narrow and overgrown, having been neglected since the previous year. As they climbed upward, they had to fight their way through tall bracken, flowering goatsbeard, and a profusion of pungent cow parsnip, but eventually they reached a wide-open area where banks of foxgloves ranging from pure white to deep rose and purple spilled over into a sloping, sunlit meadow. Most of the meadow was carpeted with buttercups and daisies.

"Dad, why does Mom always call daisies, 'day's eye'?" Joel asked as they crossed the meadow.

Dad smiled. " 'Day's eye' is the flower's ancient name," he said. "People used to call it that because the flower opens its 'eye' at daybreak and closes it again at night."

At the far edge of the meadow an ingenious woodcutter had hewn a rough bench out of old Sitka spruce that had been struck by lightning many years earlier. Joel sat down, and his father joined him. Several black-chinned hummingbirds that flashed like jewels in the sun probed the hearts of red-and-yellow columbine for nectar.

"Imagine," Dad said, "the hummingbird, which only weighs half an ounce, often flies one hundred feet a second, which is more than a mile a minute. What incredible design God built into such a tiny bird!"

Dad finally got to his feet. "Well, we mustn't rest too long," he said, "or we'll get lazy and won't feel like climbing all the way to the top."

The trail narrowed again shortly after they set off, and several large stones embedded in its surface made walking difficult. After a few turns it dipped sharply and crossed a trickle of water from a spring up the hill, then rose sharply, wending its way past a small stand of shadowy spruce and tangled blackberry bushes. A sharp right turn brought them to the top of the ridge.

"What a view!" Dad said leaning over the low stone parapet built by CCC workers many years earlier. Joel and his father stared down at the gray ribbon of coastal highway along which crawled several miniature trucks and cars. Down the coast to the south they saw Heceta Head Lighthouse, the strongest light on the Oregon coast, standing watch on its rocky perch, and to the north, Yaquina Head Lighthouse that flashes a warning of danger lurking in the deceptively tranquil waters.

A car stopped in the parking lot about a hundred yards away from the lookout, and a few minutes later a young woman appeared, struggling with a sawhorse.

"Hi!" she said. "Quite a view, isn't it?"

"Yes, it is," Joel said. "But what are you doing with that thing all the way up here?"

"I'm putting the finishing touches on my carving," she said. "Come and see it. I'm very proud of it, and I'm sure you'll understand why when you see it."

Joel followed the girl up the trail till it divided. At the fork, the graceful oak carving of a slender woman, about ten feet tall, gazed with sightless eyes across the broad Pacific, her arms stretched skyward, her feet springing from a solid wood foundation. A moment later Joel's father joined them.

"I came up here to give her one last coat of preservative before leaving on a trip to the Midwest," the girl explained, placing the sawhorse in position. "Hold on a minute while I get the oil and a brush from the car."

Soon she was back. Joel and his father sat on a stony outcropping and watched while she applied the preservative. When she had finished she climbed down from her perch, replaced the lid on the can, and sat down beside them, staring up at the carving in rapt admiration.

"Well, what do you think?" she asked at last. "Beautiful, isn't she?"

"She sure is," Joel's father said quietly. "Does she have a name?"

"I've named her The Spirit of the Forest," the girl said, "because she sprang from an oak tree and represents the triumph of the spirit over adversity."

"Where did you get that idea for a name?" Joel asked.

"I was born with crippled feet," the girl replied. "After a series of operations, plus the loving care of my parents who spent hours teaching me how to walk, I was able to overcome my handicap, and now I can walk as well as anybody." She paused. "I've been thinking about a project like this for years," she said quietly. "Then one day when I was up here alone, disgusted that so many trees had fallen and been left to rot, I made up my mind I would turn one of them into something beautiful and lasting, something I could show my grandchildren."

"That's neat," Joel said. "How long did it take to carve her?"

"Almost two years," she said. "You see, it's all done by chisel, and that requires great care and concentration. One false move would have ruined the whole project."

"How did you get her up this far?" Joel asked.

"I carved her in the art department at the university," the girl explained. "It took a dozen of us to load her into the truck, carefully wrapped in burlap. I drove her to the parking lot, and they helped me carry her in from there. The rangers helped us set her in the hole we'd prepared earlier." She pointed to the base of the carving. "The hole must have been at least four feet deep, and while three of my friends held her in position, the rest put in reinforcing bars and filled the hole in with concrete. She's as steady as a rock. The girl walked over and leaned all her weight against the carving. "Sometimes," she continued dreamily, "when it's very stormy and wild, I like to think of her up here in the forest, looking down across the sea at the passing ships, braving the weather. Then sometimes, although it probably sounds silly, I worry about her as a mother would worry about her child alone in the dark." She giggled.

"How long do you think she'll last in all the violent weather the lookout gets?" Joel asked.

"I hope she lasts a hundred years at least," the girl replied. "Maybe a thousand, who knows? She's old enough already, of course. The log from which she's carved was a magnificent oak tree when Captain Cook discovered this coast in 1778."

"The earth isn't going to last a thousand years," Joel said. "Did you know that Jesus is coming soon, and then there'll be a new world?"

"Do you really think so?" she asked in surprise. "Whatever makes you say that?"

"It's in the Bible," Joel assured her. "When Jesus comes no one will ever get sick again or grow old."

"Or be born with crippled feet," Dad said softly. "Imagine being in a world like that!"

"Sounds too good to be true," she said, "but I remember my grandmother telling me stories from the Bible. I loved them. She used to say that Jesus would be coming back again. Funny, I haven't thought of it in years." She jumped to her feet. "Well, I'd better be getting along. I've got to take this stuff back to the art department before I go home."

"Here, let me help you," Joel said, picking up the paint can. His father shouldered the sawhorse. "Come and see us next time you're up this way," Joel said. "We're staying at the Whispering Spruce Campground for the next two months. My parents are hosts there."

"I'll do that," she said. "I'll stop by when I get back from vacation if I can and let you tell me some more about Jesus." She stashed her tools in the back of the station wagon, and with a wave of the hand sped off down the hill.

Joel and his father returned to the carving. "It *is*

lovely, isn't it?" Joel said. "But can you imagine a person not knowing about Jesus and that He's coming again soon?"

"It's sad, but there are many who don't know," his father replied. "Perhaps what you said to her just now will cause her to think about His coming again. All these beautiful things He's given us to enjoy—the sea, the forest, birds, and flowers—won't compare to what He has prepared for those who love Him. It will be far lovelier than we can ever imagine."

They sat by The Spirit of the Forest a little while longer, until the sun colored the ocean in soft tints of gold, orange, and pink, and then stood stiffly and began the long hike home. They walked through the forest, across the trickle of water, to the meadow. Long shadows were already creeping across the meadow, closing the eyes of the pink-tipped daisies. They made their way through the tall bracken, frightening a small brown rabbit out for an evening romp, until they were once more at the bottom of the trail.

Just before reaching the trailer they met a couple of hikers—a man and a woman—plodding along the road, bowed down under heavy knapsacks.

"Good evening, may we help you?" Dad asked. "We're the hosts here. Are you looking for a tent site?"

"We sure are!" the young woman said. "You aren't full up are you? My feet are killing me, and I ache all over from carrying this pack. It must weigh forty pounds! All I can think of is lying down."

"No problem. There's lots of room," Dad said. He stepped over to a campsite that was partially hidden from the road by ferns. "How about this one?"

"Wonderful!" the man and the woman said at once. They dropped their heavy packs on the ground.

Dad held out his hand toward the man. "My name is Kermit Rogers," he said.

"We're the Cranes," the man replied. "I'm Tom and my wife is Dora."

Dad nodded. "I'm pleased to meet both of you," he said. "I'm the host at this campground so please let me know if there's anything more we can do for you." He nodded toward their trailer. "We're in the green-and-white trailer a couple of campsites down on the right," he said.

Tom slumped down on the picnic table at the front of the campsite. "We're absolutely exhausted!" he exclaimed. "Must have hiked too far our first day out."

"How far have you walked today?" Dad asked.

"About twelve miles. It was lovely to be hiking at first," Tom replied, but when it got hot we weren't sure we'd ever reach the campground. We left our pickup at Deanport so we could hike the entire Oregon coast, but I guess we overestimated our capabilities. We should have gone into training for a hike like this."

Dora dropped down on the picnic bench, peeled off her sandals and socks, and groaned. "Just look at my feet!" she said. "They're a mass of blisters. I should have listened to my mom. She told me to wear shoes and heavy socks."

"Stay where you are," Dad said sympathetically. "I'll help get the tent up, and then I'm sure you'd like a nice hot drink to cheer you up, wouldn't you?"

Soon the tent was in place. Dad asked if they'd like wood for a fire, but they confessed that the only thing they wanted, besides the hot drink, was to crawl into their sleeping bags and sleep.

Tom fetched a pan of cool water so Dora could bathe her feet, then followed Dad to the trailer for cups of hot chocolate and cookies.

"Sure there's nothing else you need?" Dad asked when Tom returned the empty cups.

"Nothing at all," Tom said. "The cookies and hot

chocolate were delicious. Thanks. You've been very kind."

"Sleep tight then," Dad said, "and I'll check on you in the morning."

Before dark a light mist crept in from the ocean and clung to the trees like thin gray veils. It swirled across the campground, blotting out the rising moon, and before the evening was over a steady drizzle had begun to fall. Sometime during the night a stiff wind began to blow. It whipped last year's remaining dead leaves off the trees and sent them scurrying down the road. It snatched the slender catkins from the alders and showered the ground with twigs and pine tree tips. It brought rain as it gained strength, in slow measured drops at first, spattering against the trailer windows, then harder and harder. The large alder at the back of the trailer bowed deeply with each gust and tapped insistently on the roof.

The wind let up, and the rain had eased to a steady drip by the time daylight arrived, so Dad slogged off to check on Tom and Dora in their waterlogged tent. Tom was outside, gloomily surveying the sodden landscape.

"My wife's still in bed," he said. "She feels quite ill, and her feet are so swollen she can't get her shoes on." He told Dad that he had decided to hitchhike back to Deanport, pick up the truck, and find a motel until Dora's feet got better. "We can't possibly do any more walking," he said. "Must've been mad to think of hiking the coast in the first place. And what a night! I don't believe we slept more than a couple of hours, and several times I was afraid the tent would blow away. Everything we brought is soaking wet." He paused. "Guess I won't be cooking breakfast outside either. But do you think we could have another cup of hot chocolate? Then I'll be off."

"You certainly can," Dad said, "and don't worry

about fixing breakfast. My wife is cooking it right now. Come with me. We'll fix up a tray, and you can take it back with you."

In a very short time Mom had heaped two plates with scrambled eggs, crisp, hot, buttered toast, and steaming cups of hot chocolate to take back to the tent. When Tom returned he said Dora felt much better after breakfast. "We're especially thankful for the kindness of people we'd never met before," he said.

"When she feels like getting up, bring her over to the trailer," Dad told him. "She'll be warm and comfortable here, and I'll drive you over to Deanport so you can pick up your truck."

During their absence Joel took down the tent and packed the rest of their gear while Mom bathed Dora's swollen feet and applied salve and band-aids to her blisters. When Dad and Tom returned from town she fixed everyone a bowl of hot soup with homemade bread, and Dad offered a prayer for their safety on the road.

"How can we ever repay you?" Tom and Dora asked.

Dad smiled. "Just pass on the kindness to somebody else," he said.

A heavy rain began to fall again in the early afternoon, beating down the stately purple foxgloves and flattening the fragile California poppies. The rain-soaked daisies forgot to open their eyes, and the yellow Scotch broom bowed beneath the downpour. A million tiny Niagaras rushed down the hills, and the placid streams widened and roared as they rushed madly on to the sea. A dead spruce, weakened by the onslaught of generations of woodpeckers, fell to the forest floor with a crash, and a score of crows rose in a flock to protest the outrage.

"Now I know how Noah must have felt," Joel said gloomily twenty-four hours later. "I've almost forgotten what it's like to have dry, sunny weather."

"Forests need lots of rain to grow," Dad said. "I'm just glad that Tom and Dora went back to Deanport. This weather isn't even fit for a duck!"

The rain finally ceased, and the wind settled down to an apologetic murmur, gently shaking the great tree branches and sending little cascades of water onto the ground. Late in the afternoon the sun peeked down at the destruction, brightened, and set about its task of drying out the world.

Mom, Dad, and Joel put on rain boots and started off through the park to see what they could do to help. Already, nature was busy at work, lifting the sodden daisies out of the mud, encouraging the tattered foxgloves to stand tall again, inviting the bees to renew their endless quest for nectar. Banana slugs oozed noiselessly out of their hiding places. A reddish-brown nightcrawler, blind and deaf, ventured above ground, only to be seized by a hungry robin. Half its body broke away and was borne aloft to a nest of fledglings, while the other half fell back to the ground. A mole set about repairing its tunnels, and a red-spotted garter snake slithered through the wet grass in search of an insect dinner.

Joel and his parents entered a stretch of yellow broom on which raindrops still trembled. A young fawn rose from the grass, stared at them for a moment with its huge liquid brown eyes, and disappeared into the bushes on delicate high heels. A nervous brush rabbit scuttled out of the bushes to graze, changed its mind, and disappeared again. The sun shone brighter, causing wisps of steam to rise from the soaked soil, the last clouds hurried out of the sky, and hundreds of birds sang their hearts out in praise of their Creator.

Joel squinted up at Orcas Lookout, where he could faintly see the slender figure of The Spirit of the Forest, her hands stretched heavenward. "She's still there, Dad," he said, "I was afraid the storm might have toppled her."

They continued their walk, picking up dead branches that littered the campground and replacing errant garbage-can lids. Finally they returned home, wiped off the car and trailer, and opened the windows wide to let in the sunshine and the exotic scents of forest and ocean.

Tranquility had returned to Whispering Spruce Campground.

Chapter 4
Harvey's Struggle for Life

A big black crow flapped noisily from tree to tree holding reveille. Harvey, the rabbit, glanced up for a second, twitched a delicate nostril disdainfully, and continued grazing on sweet red clover by his favorite clump of salal bushes. Harvey was a domesticated rabbit, who, tired of captivity in the pen of a nearby farm, had escaped two years earlier and lived contentedly in the forest campground, where he had become almost an institution. Unlike the little brown cottontails that froze whenever a visitor walked by and then scurried off to safety in the underbrush, Harvey grazed out in the open and fearlessly allowed people to talk to him and take his photograph.

The crow continued its rounds of the campsite, waking sleepers in their tents, then winged its way back to the crow colony in the tall pine trees to recruit others to join him. But the rest had other things to do, so he returned to the campground and resumed his self-appointed task of rousing everyone to see what a splendid day it was. One camper, busily coaxing a sluggish fire into life, threw a pine cone at the crow. The cone missed him by miles, and the crow cackled in laughter.

"Hi! Harvey," Joel called, treading gently across the

dewy grass. "Having a good breakfast?"

Harvey cocked a bright brown eye in Joel's direction and resumed eating. A chipmunk ran down a branch of the salal bush, shaking dewdrops from its pale pink lanterns, and began to feast on the seeds of wild grasses, then with a flick of its striped tail disappeared into the bushes.

Mrs. Fleck in space 29 opened her trailer door softly so that Chris, her fat dachshund, could use the nearby bushes without detection. He spied Harvey at breakfast and, ignoring the pleadings of his mistress, waddled off to pick a fight. But Harvey hopped away before he even got near. Chris sniffed around for a few minutes, went on about his business, and then returned to his adoring mistress.

"I thought all dogs were supposed to be leashed, Dad," Joel said. "Why isn't he?"

"They are," his father said, "but unfortunately some people, like Mrs. Fleck, choose to ignore the rules. It's too bad, because a dog on the loose can injure our wild creatures, and, of course, they themselves run the risk of getting rabies should they be bitten by a rabid squirrel or chipmunk."

After finishing their early-morning check of the campground, Joel and his father returned home for breakfast. Later in the morning Mom asked Joel if he'd like to walk over to Benton's farm for fresh eggs and vegetables. Joel loved to visit Benton's farm with its herd of well-fed Holstein cows grazing in the lush green pastures. And what a variety of animals wandered about the place! Horses, dogs, cats, geese, and ducks. Joel loved them all. He first looked for Mrs. Benton in the airy, cool barn, then in the spotless milking shed, and finally discovered her trimming the purple wisteria that hung low over the back porch.

"Just let me finish this," she said, "and then I'll go

around the farm with you. Of course, if you'd like you're more than welcome to gather your own eggs."

Joel went over to the chicken house, and as soon as he pushed open the door the hens set up such a cackling that he yelled at them to be quiet. Of course they ignored him. Taking a large wicker basket off a shelf on the wall he started gathering the fat brown eggs, pushing aside the inquisitive hens that pecked at his legs and flapped their wings noisily. One silly hen sat in the feeder watching everything that was going on in the hen house with bright eyes and occasionally bursting out with a ridiculous cackle.

"Look at that old hen," Mrs. Benton said as she came in the door. "She's as crazy as can be. This spring she took it into her head that she wanted to raise a family, and for an entire week she sat on a plastic egg like a queen on her throne. Each morning I lifted her up and put her over the fence, and she'd stagger off muttering to herself, so one day I took the nest egg away. That didn't bother her a bit, because she went right on sitting in the same place on the ground. Then I put her in another pen, and she found an old shoe and sat on that, determined to hatch it!"

Mrs. Benton paused and shook her head. "Just last week she discovered one of my little bantams sitting on four eggs, and without so much as an 'excuse me' she sat down, right on top of the bantam, eggs, nest, and all. She can't get it into her silly head that she'll never be able to raise a family. Now she sits in the feeder all day, squawking whenever the others come near her."

A stately peacock strutted by outside, sweeping the yard with its magnificent plumage. It turned its head this way and that, looking everywhere. Suddenly it scuttled up a low bank, gave its peculiar shriek, and stood with its feathers spread like a fan while the hens stared enviously.

"It's gorgeous," Joel said in admiration. "It must be the most beautiful bird in the whole world."

"I'm sure it is," Mrs. Benton said. "In fact King Solomon kept peacocks in his palaces, and they must have been constant reminders to him that God loves beautiful things. Funny thing though," she went on, "some of the most beautiful birds such as the peacock and the parrot can't sing a note. That gift has been given to less showy birds such as the somber-hued thrush and skylark—the law of compensation, I suppose."

At that moment a golden pheasant gave an uncanny shriek. Mrs. Benton laughed. "See what I mean. It is gorgeous, but its voice is the harshest sound in the world."

Joel went over to the sheep pen and petted a lamb that was still wobbly on its legs. Its mother looked on warily from her bed of straw and bleated a caution not to hurt her baby. A couple of calves came to the fence to nuzzle Joel's hand and nibble at the hay he offered them. A family of ducks that had been sharing their pen waddled by, quacking importantly.

In the vegetable garden Joel filled a large box with luscious red strawberries, dreaming all the while of shortcake and whipped cream. Then he pulled baby carrots and clusters of tiny new potatoes.

In the orchard nearby Mrs. Benton examined the hard green knobs on the trees. "Looks as though we'll have a good crop of apples this year," she said. "And we have plenty of ripe cherries too. You'd better pick some before the birds get them all. They love cherries, you know."

The warm sunshine brought out the sweet smell of newly mown hay. Joel watched Mr. Benton as he maneuvered the mower round and round the field. The pale green hay dropped evenly to the ground as the blade passed by.

"Well, I'd better be getting home," Joel said regretfully. "Mom needs the vegetables for lunch."

But when he got back to the campsite his parents weren't there. He looked around and on the picnic table he found a cardboard box, sealed with wide tape. A note attached to the side said, "Hi! I'm Harvey, the rabbit. I've been injured and am in pain. I need lots of love and attention. Please help me."

A little red-headed boy came over to the picnic table. "It was that dachshund," he said. "He was outside without his leash, and he crept up on Harvey. They got into a fight, and Harvey didn't stand a chance. The dachshund bit his ear and tore his coat and he's bleeding a lot. We didn't know what to do, so my dad told me to bring him over here to you, that *you'd* know what to do. I gave him a lettuce leaf, but he didn't eat it."

Joel pulled off the tape and opened the lid. Harvey crouched, trembling, in the corner of the box. His chest heaved in shallow gasps. Joel ran inside and fetched a dish of cool water. Back outside, he stroked Harvey's silken head, telling him he'd be all right.

"You're safe, Harvey," he said over and over. "Don't worry, that horrid dog won't get to you again. I'll make sure of that. Dad will be home soon, and he'll make you feel better."

Dad was very upset when he returned and learned what had happened. "Are you positive that Mrs. Fleck's dachshund is the culprit?" he asked the boy.

"Yes," came the firm reply, "and my dad saw it too."

Dad marched over to Mrs. Fleck's trailer. She was lying outside on a deck chair reading when he arrived, and she greeted him with a bright smile.

"Lovely day, isn't it?" she said. "I decided to work on my tan a bit while Chris recovers from a nasty shock he had this morning. Poor little sweetie pie. A thing like that does upset him so; he has such a delicate temperament. I don't know if you heard, but that horrid rabbit came right over here and attacked my darling doggie who was just minding his own business, weren't you, sweetie pie?"

Chris thumped his stubby tail on the grass and slobbered.

"I'm very vexed with Chris," Dad said, trying to keep his voice calm. "I understand that you let him outside this morning, and he attacked Harvey and hurt him badly. You know the park rules, Mrs. Fleck. Dogs must be on a leash at all times, and you deliberately broke that rule."

"Chris wouldn't attack anything, would you, sweetie pie?" Mrs. Fleck cooed, kneading the dachshund's fat wrinkled neck. "Chris only went for a tiny walk and came right back again. If there was a fight it was all Harvey's fault."

"Chris was seen attacking Harvey," Dad said firmly. "In the future, Mrs. Fleck, please restrain your dog when you're in this campground, or you'll be asked to leave."

"I don't care about your silly rabbit," she snapped, getting up from the deck chair and stalking over to her trailer. "There are scores of rabbits around here, and they're regular pests."

"Harvey is not an ordinary rabbit," Dad said quietly. "He is almost the park mascot. We all love him, especially the children, and he's never harmed anything in his life. Mrs. Fleck, keep that dog on its leash."

"I hope I wasn't too hard on her," Dad said when he returned to the trailer, "but she really vexed me. But now that it's off my chest, we must do something for poor Harvey."

"I have an idea, Dad," Joel said. "Let's take him over to Mrs. Benton's. She keeps rabbits, and she'll know what to do."

Joel held the box while he and his father walked over to the farm. Mrs. Benton took Harvey out gently, laid him on a bed of straw, and examined him carefully.

"There are no broken bones that I can tell," she began, "but he doesn't look good. He's badly torn, and besides that he's received a terrible shock and lost a lot of blood. I'll doctor him up the best I can. Right now he needs peace and quiet more than anything else."

She stroked the rabbit's trembling head, and Harvey shivered and looked up with pain-filled eyes.

"Try not to worry about Harvey," she told Joel as they left. "I'll give him the best of care, and I'll come by to see you in the morning to let you know how he's getting along. Then you can come over to visit him if you like."

Mrs. Benton came by about 7:30 the next morning. "I'm sorry," she said, "but when I got up to check on Harvey during the night he was dead. I did all I could for him, but I guess it wasn't enough. I'm very sorry, Joel. I know how much you cared for him."

"I hate Mrs. Fleck and that stupid Chris," he stormed after Mrs. Benton had left. "Why don't you tell them to get out of the park before he kills something else?"

"I know how you feel, Son," his father said. "But you mustn't hate her. I guess she doesn't know any better. And Chris was only doing what comes naturally to a dog. They're born hunters, you know."

Mom tried to comfort Joel. She reminded him that in the New World there won't be any fierce animals to kill or destroy. The lion will lie down with the lamb, and nothing will ever be harmed.

After breakfast Joel walked sadly over to Mrs. Benton's farm. He picked up the box containing what remained of Harvey and carried him home. Dad had dug a shallow grave under the pink-blossomed salal bushes he loved so much, and they buried him. Each morning as the family made their rounds of the campground Joel thought of Harvey and how he had loved the dewy mornings and the sweet red clover, and in his heart he felt very sad. And he always tried to avoid space 29.

At the end of the campground was a bog where the bright yellow skunk cabbage flourished, along with the exotic *Darlingtonia* or pitcher plant, whose cobralike hood lures to certain death any unwary insect that is rash enough to venture near its trap.

As Joel returned from the playground one evening he heard a growling and snorting in the bog, and he stopped to investigate. To his horror he saw Chris rooting around the edges of the bog, trampling the pitcher plants in an effort to flush out a brown cottontail.

"Get out of there, you bad dog," he yelled. "Haven't you learned your lesson yet? Get away from those plants. Go home!"

Chris continued snorting and digging, but suddenly the rabbit took off down the path, and Chris waddled after it. The cottontail disappeared into the trees, but then Chris surprised a chipmunk at its evening meal and rushed down the path after it, along a wooden pier. Suddenly to his total surprise, Chris fell feet first into a dark pond. The chipmunk watched from a nearby log. Chris tried to swim, but his long heavy body kept going under the surface of the water. He made a gallant attempt at striking out with his powerful front legs, but fatigue finally forced him to give up the struggle. He floundered about for a desperate minute and then sank.

Joel leaped into the water, grabbed Chris by the collar, hauled him out of the water, and dumped him on the bank. Chris coughed, shook his coat, bared his teeth, and slunk off toward home, strands of muddy grass trailing behind him.

Joel wiped the water out of his eyes and walked back to the campground with water streaming from clothes. As he passed Mrs. Fleck's trailer he heard her exclaiming that her sweetie pie was all wet, and what nasty animal had tricked him into going in the water, and she must get him dried off before he caught his death of cold.

"Where have you been?" Mom gasped when she saw Joel's sorry state. "What happened? Hurry inside and get out of those filthy, wet clothes and into a hot shower."

"I was walking home from the playground and saw Chris," Joel muttered through chattering teeth. "He was off his leash again, rooting about on the edge of the bog. That's where I saw him first, and then he started chasing a chipmunk and didn't even notice where he was going and fell right off the end of the pier into Black Pond. You should have see him floundering about!" Joel laughed in spite of his chattering teeth. "He couldn't swim, so I jumped in and fished him out."

"You jumped in?" his father exclaimed. "I thought you detested him." He paused. "Actually, I'm glad you did it, Son. I'm proud of you. You were able to forgive your enemy, and that's the important thing. And Chris doesn't deserve to die just because he's a spoiled dog that belongs to a foolish woman who refuses to obey the park rules and keep him on a leash. While you get into the shower, I'm off to have a talk with the woman in question and tell her I expect her and her dog to be out of here by tomorrow morning."

Mrs. Fleck was already hooking up as they made their rounds of the campground the next day. Chris bared his teeth at Joel and snarled nastily when they stopped to speak.

"Good morning, Mrs. Fleck," Dad said pleasantly. "I'm sorry your vacation had to end like this. "Nevertheless, I hope you have a safe journey. Here, let me help you with that jack." Mrs. Fleck ignored him.

"Come along, sweetie pie," she said to Chris. "I know you don't like this place any more than I do. We're going to find a place where they appreciate a nice doggie like you."

"I hope you find what you're looking for," Dad said. "But most of all, please keep Chris on a leash while you're in the forest. He has already cost the life of Harvey and given Joel a cold bath as well."

Mrs. Fleck sniffed. "Oh, yes, I meant to thank you, Joel, for helping him out of the pond last evening. Mr. Simpson told me what you did. He saw the whole thing, apparently. Poor Chris doesn't always watch where he's going, and he thanks you too, don't you, sweetie pie?"

Chris bared his teeth again and slunk around behind Mrs. Fleck and growled. He wasn't in the habit of thanking anybody—not even his doting mistress.

Chapter 5
Captured!

One by one the campfires flickered and died, leaving nothing but little heaps of soft gray ash. The summer visitors, filled with roasted hot dogs and marshmallows, retired to their campers and sleeping bags, to be lulled to sleep by the soft breeze that played in the topmost branches of the giant spruce and pine. A pale moon sailed majestically across the dark sky, looking down on a world where everything slept.

But not everything.

The evening bat, with its insatiable appetite still unappeased after a long winter of hibernation, flew with unerring accuracy through the forest, guided by its sonar. It caught midges, flies, and mosquitoes and tossed them into its tail membranes with powerful wings. Without its massive consumption of these pests, life in the campground would have been considerably less comfortable.

A full orchestra of frogs tuned up for their nightly symphony, and a skunk emerged from its burrow under a rotting log to satisfy its hunger for fruits, small snakes, and, if fortunate enough to locate an unguarded nest, bird eggs.

A bandit-faced raccoon leaped out of its hiding place

in a snag and took a tour of the campground. Familiar with human beings and their ways, it knew it had nothing to fear. It had developed a taste for the food that people often left laying around carelessly. Near one of the tents it spied a half-eaten cob of buttered corn, picked it up in its paws, and nibbled at the sweet kernels. Next came a fried chicken bone, and for dessert an apple core. Then, frustrated that the campers were less wasteful than usual, the raccoon ran to the nearest garbage can and rattled it angrily.

Half a mile away a mother bear woke suddenly. She peered with piglike eyes through the ferns in her forest hideaway and clumsily raised her huge body to an upright position. Under a thin coating of pine needles she spied a fragrant pink mushroom and licked it up with her tongue. She looked over at her two sleeping cubs. They had gotten quite tired the day before learning the bear survival tricks she taught them and were snoring lustily, so she went over to a little stream that cascaded through the rocks and dipped in a paw.

Hearing the whimper of one of the cubs, the mother bear hurried back, but instead of comforting it she swatted it across the head with her paw. The cub had wakened with an empty stomach and wanted milk, but instead it received an immediate lesson on foraging for ants in a nearby hill.

Both cubs were overdue for weaning. The mother bear pushed her way through the forest, the two cubs trailing behind her, complaining all the way, until at last the three of them stood at the very rim of the campground. Visions of the food humans ate—bacon rind and watermelons, jam and honeyed bread—made her bold, but the greedy raccoon had left nothing. Angrily, she lumbered over to a garbage can by the first restroom, and standing on her powerful back legs, ripped off the lid and dumped everything on the ground. The cubs watched with interest from the shadows as she grabbed a half-eaten bread roll, a grease-soaked paper wrapping, and a discarded baked potato. She dropped a cantalope rind on the ground beside the can, and the cubs made a rush for it. They fought, punched, and rolled until she cuffed them both across the ears. Then she ate the rind herself.

Leaving a trail of papers behind her, she lumbered off to the next garbage can just in time to surprise a middle-aged woman in her dressing gown who was paying a nighttime visit to the restroom. The woman screamed, fled back down the path, burst into her tent, and collapsed in a trembling heap beside her sleeping husband.

When the bear recovered from her fright, she impressed on her cubs the lesson that human beings are to be avoided at all costs. The next garbage can lid crashed to the ground, and the mother bear again rooted through the rubbish, searching for food. From one garbage can to the next she went, till she'd made the rounds of the campground, only then returning to her forest home, her two cubs still trailing behind.

Attracted by the bright lights of the restrooms, a thousand moths fluttered and beat their wings against the glass, perishing in the process until the ground was littered with broken bodies.

A grayish-brown mouse climbed into one of the plastic bags in an overturned garbage receptacle to feast on discarded fruit and other household scraps, till finally, stuffed full, it fell asleep, its soft body slumped over a soggy bread roll. Some time later the mouse awoke, and finding no way out of its plastic supermarket, spent the night racing around the bag trying to get out. Finally, forgetting how it got in, it began chewing at the plastic bag until it had made a hole big enough to squeeze through. Then it raced to the edge of the overturned garbage can, ran around the outside a couple of times, and scampered back into the plastic bag for more food.

A thrush, attracted by the lights, flew into one of the restrooms, fluttered about for a second or two, and finally settled on a beam several feet above the floor. The bird managed to dislocate a tiny spider spinning a silvery thread across the window and routed a big black ant from the corner before deciding to resume her flight home. She flew up to the skylight, but though she beat her wings frantically against it, she found no way to the outside. She swooped low across the room seeking the exit, and round and round. Fear caused her to soil the walls and floor with dark berry stains. Finally, utterly exhausted and her heart racing with fear, she gave up and huddled on the beam again. She could find no way out of the trap.

Gradually the moon slipped out of sight, making way for the morning sun. The bats had long since returned to their trees, the skunk and raccoon to their burrows. The mother bear and her cubs were safe in their ferny beds, to sleep the summer day away.

After sunup Joel and his father began their morning rounds while Mom worked around the trailer. Presently they came upon the first overturned garbage can with its clutter of papers and other rubbish.

"Whatever's happened?" Joel asked, spearing the papers with his stick. "What a mess! Whoever did it?"

"Whatever did it, you mean?" Dad said. "Looks like we had a visit from a bear last night. See how the garbage has been dragged through the bushes and up the hill? He left his calling card in the mud as well."

They righted the can, gathered up the garbage, and continued on down the road, where they found that other cans had been vandalized in similar fashion. One of the campers called to them from his tent, and they went over to see what was the matter.

"My wife had quite a fright last night," he said. "Claims she met an enormous bear on the path to the restroom. It scared her half to death, and she insists we get out of here while we're still alive. Have you seen any bears about at all?"

"We haven't *seen* any," Dad said, "but there's enough evidence to indicate one paid us a visit last night and rummaged through the garbage cans. I'm sorry it scared your wife, although I'm sure she had nothing to fear. They're more scared of us than we are of them. They make nuisances of themselves around camp-grounds, I know, especially if they've acquired a taste for the things we eat."

"You should have seen it!" the woman said, sticking her head out of the tent flap. "It was huge! I told Herb that I'm not staying any place where a person can't even go to the washroom without meeting something like that on the way! I'm lucky to be alive to tell the story, I am."

"I'll report it to the ranger," Dad said, "and once again, I'm sorry you had such a fright."

They continued on their rounds. Joel stepped into one of the restrooms to check the paper and soap sup-ply. Suddenly he stopped and looked at the walls and the floor, then went back outside.

"There's something strange in there, Dad," he said. "Come and see. There are stains down the walls and on the floor. Whatever can it be?"

"I have no idea," his father said, looking all around the room, "but I'll get the hose and clean the place up." Then he glanced up at the ceiling. "Poor little thing," he said, calling softly to the thrush perched on the beam. "Come on down, little bird, come on down. We won't hurt you. You can't stay up there for ever, you know; you must be terribly thirsty." But the bird didn't move from its perch.

Dad scrubbed down the walls and took a hose to the floor while the little bird watched with glazed eyes.

"I know, I'll see if I can pry her loose with the broom," Joel said. He hurried off to the storage area. A moment later he returned. Carefully he pushed the broom in the direction of the bird, but with a terrified screech she swooped across the room to avoid this strange new threat. Then she flew back to her perch on the beam.

"I'm only trying to help you," Joel said softly. "I won't hurt you. Look, here's the door, the way you came in. Please fly out again."

"Put the broom back, Joel," Dad said. "That won't work. We're scaring the poor creature more than helping it. But if it stays up there it'll either die from lack of water or from fright. Maybe I can find a ladder and coax it down." He hurried off to the storage area.

Joel had a better idea. He closed his eyes and said, "Dear Jesus, You know there's a little bird in here, and it can't find its way out again. We don't want it to die. Please show it the way out."

When Dad returned he said he couldn't find a ladder, but in any case, he doubted it would do much good because as soon as he got near, the bird would fly away in a panic and quite possibly injure itself or die of a heart attack. "All we can do is leave and hope it finds the door eventually," he said.

"I have an idea!" Joel said. "It might just work."

He went outside to a bush with bright salmonberries that hung low over the path. Gathering a dozen of the plumpest berries, he took them into the restroom. He laid one on a low shelf where the bird would be sure to see it, another some distance away, and the last one just inside the door. "When she sees these," he said, "maybe she'll follow the berry trail right out the door. I know it will work. It must!"

The bird stared at the brightly colored fruit, cocked

its head, and fluttered down to the shelf. Joel and his father slipped noiselessly out of the door and continued on with their other work. When they checked the restrooms half an hour later, the only reminder that a bird had been imprisoned there all night was the trail of half-eaten salmonberries.

"Thank You, Jesus," Joel said softly as he wiped up the remains of the fruit. "Thank You for showing a little bird the way home."

The mother bear woke up from her day-long nap and yawned. She felt weary at her cub's incessant clamor for milk that she no longer intended to give them. Her stomach was empty, and she thought of the garbage cans where there was plenty of food with almost no work to get it. Perhaps it would be all right to leave her cubs for one night. They needed to learn how to fend for themselves. They needed to use the lessons she had tried to teach them. So she rose to her feet and padded noiselessly through the tall bracken to the campground. As she walked, the breeze carried a tantalizing odor to her nose that made her mouth water. She twitched her nose, sniffing the air as she lumbered on down the path. The scent grew so strong that she almost choked with desire, and heedless of where she was going, lurched forward and snatched at a hunk of rotting deer meat, richly coated with a thick layer of choice white maggots. She tore hungrily at the meat, pausing only to wipe the maggots from her muzzle with her paw. She took two more steps forward to snatch another piece of meat, and a heavy iron gate fell behind her.

Something struck a cord in her slow mind. She heard the faint cry of one of her cubs, and she moved to turn, but she could go neither forward nor back. She snorted with rage and frustration, thrashing around in the close confines of the trap, and finally with a moan of despair sank her massive head onto her front paws. Far away she heard the other cub cry, and she bawled. Man had tricked her, and she had been a willing victim.

When the morning sun chased the pale moon out of the sky, she peered through the bars with bloodshot eyes, wondering where she was. She felt very thirsty and longed for her cool forest stream.

About the middle of the day a jeep drove up, and a ranger jumped out, followed by Joel and his father. "Look at that," the ranger gloated. "Caught first time we had the trap out. That's what caused such a mess in the campground the other night and scared a poor woman half to death."

They walked over to the bear trap, and keeping a safe distance, looked inside. Mother bear stuck a bruised paw up to the bars, grunted, and stared out with tiny hate-filled eyes. She recognized the scent of man and feared it.

A little later the ranger returned with a tractor and attached it to the bear trap. With much bumping and swerving he hauled it several miles into the hills and then opened the back gate. Mother bear stumbled out, moaning for her bruised body and for her cubs. She headed into the underbrush to lick her wounds. Exhausted, she lay down on the soft pine needles, put her head on her paws, and fell asleep.

That night she quenched her raging thirst in a crystal clear pond, then set out in search of her cubs, but by the time she found them, they wanted nothing more to do with her. She had deserted them, they thought, and in so doing had broken the bonds that tie a mother to her offspring.

Her longing for human food outweighed her fear of man, and before the summer was over she was back in the campground, pawing through garbage cans again.

Chapter 6

Fire at Whispering Spruce Campground

The campground had already begun to fill up with motor homes, campers, trucks, and trailers by midafternoon on the third of July. Scores of children spilled across the campground, joined by an assortment of dogs and cats, all anxious to explore their new surroundings while their parents set up for the long weekend. The children and their pets shouted and barked with glee at their new-found freedom.

A wood vendor kept busy supplying bundles of cedar for the fires that sprang up all around the campground. A ball game started up in the group picnic area, and a family reunion got underway in a meadow underneath a giant spruce. A lone cyclist set up his tent in a secluded nook, sat on a pine log, and tuned up his violin.

By the time evening had spread a thin veil of mist over the tall trees, the campground was full, so Dad placed a "CAMP FULL" sign by the entrance. Still, several other campers came by seeking admission. As it grew dark most of the campers retired one by one to their tents and trailers. But a few, disregarding the "NO FIREWORKS" signs posted at every restroom, shattered the quiet with pops and cracks that sent streams of brightly colored sparks high into the air and woke every dog in the camp.

"I wish they wouldn't do that," Dad said uneasily, wondering if he should tell them to stop but not wishing to spoil their fun. But at last even the fireworks ended.

The following day was livelier than ever, and the Stars and Stripes appeared at almost every campsite. The air was filled with the shrieks of happy children cycling up and down the pathways, playing ball, splashing in the little creek, and chasing each other up and down the trails. Finally, stuffed with charred hot dogs, sweet corn, and ice-cold watermelon, the people lay around in the sunshine to read, sleep, or talk.

Later, many of them went into the nearby town to visit the stalls, ride on the swings and merry-go-rounds, and, as if they hadn't eaten enough at lunchtime, to snack on huge blobs of cotton candy, ice cream, or hot buttered popcorn. Most stayed to watch the fireworks display on the town's sandy beach and didn't return until long after dark.

The parents of a family of small boys asked Dad if he thought it would be all right to let off a few fireworks in the evening, as the children were too young to be kept out of their beds to watch the ones in town. Dad suggested that they take them to the parking lot at the far end of the campground, away from the high trees and dry grass.

But somehow, as so often happens with small boys, one of them couldn't wait to set off his sparklers, and then petrified when he saw the flying sparks, threw it into the bushes. Instantly the dry underbrush burst into flames.

The child's mother screamed, grabbed her little ones, and fled to safety while her husband rushed to a pay telephone to call for help. Dad heard the screams and ran to their campsite, fastened a hose to the water faucet, and in a few minutes the fire was out. About the same time, to the wide-eyed amazement of the children, a huge red fire engine, its bell clanging wildly, tore into the campground, and half a dozen men leaped off and demanded to know where the fire was. "It's out now," Dad said, wiping a blackened hand across his forehead, "but thanks for coming anyway." After examining the grass and bushes around the area to make sure no sparks remained, the firemen left. When everything had settled back to normal, the children's father came up to Dad. "I'm very sorry this had to happen," he said. Then he turned to the children. "And now, instead of fireworks, it's bed for the lot of you." The children wailed noisily.

"Oh, don't do that," Dad said. "Boys will be boys, you know. Besides, this is the Fourth of July, a time for celebration. Tell you what. Let's all go to the parking lot and have our fireworks display, and then I'll tell a story around the campfire."

"You've all heard of Smokey the Bear, haven't you?" Dad asked the children and their parents half an hour later as they all sat around the campfire. "Now I'm going to tell you the true story of how he got that name. A long time ago, before any of you were born, there was a lovely big forest of tall trees, much like this one, where bears and deer, rabbits and raccoons lived, and where lots of fish swam in the cool streams. Brightly painted butterflies flitted among the flowers, and all kinds of birds built their nests in the trees. Oh, it was a lovely forest and home to many, many kinds of creatures.

"The summer was unusually hot and dry that year— so hot that the animals made their beds in the shade and worried that the streams might dry up, and then where would they go to drink? Even the fish were worried, because the water in their streams was getting low, and they *couldn't* leave and find another place to live. The green grass turned golden brown, the flowers wilted for lack of moisture, and the sticks and pine needles were so dry they snapped like popcorn when anything walked across them. Even the forest was no longer cool.

"Then it happened! Some careless person threw a lighted match, or perhaps a cigarette, into the forest and created a tiny spark. The spark became a flame, and the flame became a fire. Fortunately, a man in the lookout tower spotted the smoke and telephoned the ranger station, and soon firefighters and equipment were rushed into the forest. Then the wind began to blow, fanning the flames which roared into the high trees and burned up all the grass and flowers. The animals fled in terror. Some were so confused that they ran *into* the fire instead of *away* from it, and many that tried to outrun the flames died in the attempt. Others tried to hide, but it did no good. The fire found them anyway."

Dad paused and looked at the children. "The men fought the fire for almost a week, and some of them were badly burned. Many animals that had lived in the forest lost their lives, and all the birds flew away, their nests destroyed. When it was all over, instead of the once-beautiful forest, there was nothing but miles and miles of scorched, leafless trees, and the sweet piney scent had been replaced by the smell of burnt wood.

"The forest was very, very quiet. There were no birds singing in the tall trees and no bobtailed rabbits scampering about. There were no tender plants for the deer to eat and no nuts for the squirrels to hide. Even if there had been, there were no animals left to eat them or hide them. There were no little streams gurgling over the stones. The fish, the grass and the flowers, the butterflies, and the dragonflies had all died in the fire.

"As the weary firemen were about to leave the forest

and return to their homes, one of them spotted something moving on one of the trees. Looking closer, he discovered a little bear clinging to a burned tree trunk. Its mother had perished in the fire, and the baby bear was badly burned and very, very frightened. Tenderly the firemen fetched the bear down and carried him like a sick baby to a very kind game warden, who put soothing ointment on his burns and carefully bandaged his feet. The little bear missed his mother terribly, and in addition to being scared of these strange creatures that had befriended him, he was hungry and thirsty. The game warden fed the little bear, and soon his hair grew back over the burned places, and he learned to love his new friend. In time he forgot about the terrible forest fire that had killed his mother and many of his friends and destroyed his home. This story appeared in several newspapers, and he made several appearances on television, wearing a forest ranger's hat. The whole country loved this little bear that had been saved from the terrible forest fire.

"In time, Smokey, as he was called, became the symbol of fire prevention, and his picture was posted everywhere, reminding people to be very careful with fire, especially when they were out in our beautiful forests. If Smokey could speak, he would tell us much more about that terrible day, when, because of one careless person with matches, thousands and thousands of trees were destroyed, and many beautiful creatures lost their lives."

The children were very quiet when Dad had finished telling them the story of Smokey the Bear and promised never to play with fire again. Then Mom fixed hot chocolate for everybody, and soon four tired little boys were on their way home to bed.

"It's been a busy day," Dad sighed as, much later in the evening, they sat around the campfire. "I'm glad the Fourth of July comes only once a year. By this time tomorrow most of our visitors will have left, and the forest will be quiet again." He paused and smiled. "But I wouldn't have missed it for anything."

An old owl looked out of its hole in a snag and hooted at the sliver of a moon in the sky, and far away, in a secluded nook, the sweet, lilting voice of a violin played as a young man sang:

Oh Lord my God, when I in awesome wonder
Consider all the worlds Thy hands have made.
I see the stars, I hear the rolling thunder
Thy power throughout the universe displayed.
Then sings my soul, my Saviour God to Thee
How great Thou art, How great Thou art.
Then sings my soul, my Saviour God to Thee
How great Thou art, how great Thou art.

Early next morning the campers began streaming out of the forest, headed for home, though some decided to stay a day longer to avoid the rush. Dad spent a good deal of the day directing traffic while Joel picked up litter.

Mom was in the trailer baking a batch of cookies when she heard a knock at the door. It was a young woman asking if anyone had turned in a set of keys. "My name's Helen," she said. "I've lost my keys and I've searched everywhere, but they're nowhere to be found. We've got to leave right after lunch, but without the keys we won't get very far."

Mom asked if she'd checked the restrooms and every other place where she might have been.

"Yes, everywhere," Helen said in desperation. "At first I thought my children might have gotten hold of them, but they assured me they haven't touched them. Then I thought of you, hoping someone might have handed them in. Oh dear, I've got to find them! They're the keys to the car—the only set we have with us."

"I'll come help you look again," Mom said. "I'm good at finding things. Just ask my husband—all except my glasses," she added with a giggle. "I'm always losing them and asking him to help me search for them."

Mom walked over to Helen's campsite and began looking around. "I know they're not here," Helen said again. "My husband and I have both searched every blade of grass and every bush in the area. The keys vanished into thin air."

As Mom walked up and down the campsite she kept her eyes on the ground, searching everywhere, and suddenly she caught a glint of metal in the tall grass. She bent down and picked up a bunch of keys!

"But we searched that spot several times," Helen said in amazement. "How clever of you to find them, and so quickly too!" Thanks so much. I don't know what we'd have done, because we'd planned on leaving directly after lunch."

At supper that evening Mom told the story of the lost keys. "It was the strangest thing," she began. "She was telling me about their electronics business, and she added that her husband closes it down from sunset on Friday till sunset on Saturday. 'You'll probably wonder why,' she told me, 'but we believe that God wants us to keep the Sabbath from sunset to sunset, not on Sunday.'

Mom smiled. "You should have seen her surprised look when I told her we keep the Sabbath too. I asked her if they were Seventh-day Adventists, and she said No; they didn't believe in any organized religion. I invited her to visit our church one day. While she didn't promise anything, she didn't say No, either. Before they left I gave her a *Steps to Christ*. What's more, she said they expect to be back here in a few weeks for their summer vacation and promised to visit with us."

"That's extraordinary," Dad said. "If she hadn't lost her keys you would never have met her, and neither of you would ever have known that you both keep the Sabbath."

"I had no idea, when we took this job, that hosting would be so exciting," Joel exclaimed.

It was quiet when Joel and his parents made their evening rounds. As they walked home, softly through the dim forest they heard the violin in another of its nocturnal concerts. When the last notes had died away, all that could be heard was the soft melody of the wind in the trees, the murmur of the ocean, and the splashing of the ever-flowing stream.

Chapter 7
Timbu

"Qui, qui, quiro," chattered the chickaree squirrel angrily as he nibbled on a mushroom he had hidden in the moss of his nest to dry. Twice he had been interrupted in his hunt for soft mosses with which to line his nest, first by an inquisitive blue jay looking for seeds and then by a strange colored object that fluttered down from the skies and landed at the foot of his favorite spruce tree.

The squirrel finished the mushroom, leaped to the ground, and unearthed one of the cones he had stored away the previous autumn, then raced back to his nest with the cone in his mouth. Holding the cone in his paws, he stripped away the scales with his sharp little teeth to get at the seeds and dropped the rest on the ground.

Still chattering, the squirrel sprang from one branch to another, then leaped to the ground and raced to another tree, stopping to make sure he wouldn't meet an enemy before swinging through the branches. He still must find soft mosses for his nest before the other squirrels got them, for in another few weeks it would be time to gather nuts and cones again and hide them where only he would know where they were.

But for now the sun shone warmly on the tall spruce, a little breeze rocked the bough where he rested, and he began to feel ever so sleepy. So, giving way to unaccustomed laziness, he rolled himself up into a ball, covered his body with his bushy tail, and fell asleep.

A crashing sound in the forest far below woke him up. No animal ever made a noise like that, especially in the middle of the day, except perhaps one of those uncivilized dogs from the campground. He uncurled himself and with one bound was out of the nest, leaping through the trees, scolding all the way.

It was Joel, pushing his way up the steep slope by hanging onto exposed roots and forest creepers, up, up, up, his heels digging into the loamy soil, his eye on a gaily colored kite.

Joel had seen the kite earlier that morning, fluttering over the campground on an invisible string, and he watched breathlessly as it caught the currents of wind, twisted and frolicked for a few minutes, shot up in the air, and then dived swiftly to the ground, tangled in the lowest branches of a spruce tree.

The squirrel scolded him again for intruding into his territory, but Joel was almost within reach of the kite. Then a sudden gust of wind caught the kite, shifted it ever so slightly, and the squirrel leaped up to the topmost branches, chattering angrily. Steadying himself with one hand, Joel gently extricated the kite, and clasping it closely to him, began the descent down the slope, slipping on pine needles and sliding in the soft earth, until with a final rush he was at the bottom.

A passing ranger stopped his truck and climbed out, grinning widely. "I've been watching you," he chuckled, "and wondered why you did it the hard way. If you had walked to the ridge road, you could have leaned over the bank and fished it out of the branches. It was only a couple of feet off the road."

"How was I to know?" Joel said when he told his parents about the kite at the dinner table an hour or so later. "When I saw where it had landed, I just started climbing to get it."

"I doubt the climb hurt you," his father chuckled. "Oh, and guess what. I've got some good news. The ranger stopped by this morning and asked if we'd consider staying on as hosts through to the end of August since the one who was originally coming is still in the hospital."

"What did you say?" Joel asked breathlessly as he put a spoonful of beans in his mouth.

"I told him we didn't even have to think about it this time. The answer is a unanimous Yes."

Joel's thoughts were far away as he ate his lunch, so he wasn't sure he'd heard his mother correctly when she asked if he'd like to ride a camel. Surely she must be confused, he thought, or his ears weren't working as well as usual. "Did you say something about riding a camel," he asked, "or was I dreaming?"

"No, you weren't dreaming," she giggled. "I asked if you'd like to ride a camel."

"You mean a real camel?" Joel asked. "Why, sure I would, but I doubt there's one around here."

"You'd be surprised what strange things lurk in this part of the world," she said. "But finish your lunch. We thought we'd take a drive this afternoon. Things are rather slow around the campground right now."

An hour later they drove out of the forest, past a lake as blue as the sky where masses of pink and white waterlilies served as resting places for a thousand frogs. They turned onto the coast highway that wound along a rocky shore and gradually gave way to a sandy beach. They stopped for a few minutes to examine an enormous Indian midden (refuse heap). A nearby plaque said that many years ago the Indians who lived by the sea subsisted primarily on berries and shellfish and that they piled the shells in huge heaps, some often reaching heights of forty feet or more!

The road wound inland, and the beach gave way to glistening dunes. The sun's reflection off the sand hurt their eyes. Without the cooling breezes to temper the heat it became quite uncomfortable, and there wasn't a tree in sight.

Presently, they parked their car and walked about, looking at the ever-changing sand dunes that move continuously inland in a relentless march that has almost completely buried what was once a vast evergreen forest. Strong coastal winds change and mold the dunes constantly so that they never retain the same shape for long. This constant changing is called the "Oh, no!" by dune-buggy operators. One traveling the same way he did a few hours earlier may come over a deceptively smooth crest, expecting to continue on down the other side, only to find nothing there. He may suddenly discover all four wheels clear of the sand, or he may find himself careening wildly out of control down an unexpected slip face.

Joel heard dune buggies roaring in the distance. Presently, a buggy topped the dune above them and came speeding toward them. The operator stopped and got off only a few feet from them to make an adjustment on his motor. Joel walked over, his father close behind.

"Hi," Dad said. "My name's Kermit Rogers." He held out his hand.

The man turned and smiled and shook Dad's hand. "I'm Jim," he said, and he turned back to his buggy. "This thing isn't acting right. Keeps cutting out on me."

Joel and his parents watched Jim turn the needles on his carburetor a time or two. He started to climb back

onto his buggy, then turned and asked if they had
buggies.

"No," Dad said. "We're just out walking around."

"You need to be real careful, even walking," Jim
said. "Some people become very disoriented when they
get among the dunes. They are totally surrounded by
sand, and they lose sight of every discernible land-
mark. Some people panic and would never find their
way back except for the Dune Buggy Patrol, whose job
it is to find lost travelers. When walking or riding on
the sand dunes it's advisable to carry a loud whistle, as
well as a supply of water, and if lost, not to panic but to
stay still and wait to be found," he told them.

They watched the dune buggies a while longer, and
then Mom suggested that they go in search of a camel
to ride. Sure enough, down the road they came across a
camel and its owner by the side of the road, and to Joel
it seemed as though they had suddenly been dropped
into the middle of the Sahara Desert.

Dad stopped the car, and everyone got out and
walked over to the camel that knelt on the sand, slowly
tearing lengths of alfalfa from a bundle in front of him.

"What's its name?" Joel asked the camel driver.

"Timbu. Would you like to ride him?"

Joel looked at his father, who pulled out his wallet
and paid the camel driver. The driver helped Joel get
on the camel's back.

"Come on, get up, you lazy creature," the camel
driver said. "You've got work to do." He prodded Timbu
gently.

Joel patted the camel's rough tan coat.

"Are you comfortable?" the camel driver asked after
the camel was on its feet. "Hold on tight now. Come
along, Timbu." The camel took a step. It lurched to the
left, then to the right. Left, right, left, right, like a huge
ship rolling first one way and then the other across the

sea. Joel realized why the camel is called the "ship of the desert"—not only because it is the prime means of transportation in the desert, but also because of its peculiar walking motion.

Joel talked to his parents about camels all the way back to camp. "A dune buggy may be a faster way to travel across the desert," he said, "but camels have been crossing the desert for thousands of years."

"The Bible says that Job owned 3,000 camels," Dad said.

"Camels carried Rebekah from Haran back to Canaan to be Isaac's wife," Mom added.

Joel thought a minute. "I'll bet," he said, "that the Queen of Sheba rode a camel when she went to see King Solomon!"

Dad looked at him and slapped his knee. "I'll bet you're right, Son," he said.

That night Joel went to sleep pretending he was crossing the Sahara Desert swaying back and forth on a camel's back.

Chapter 8

Invasion at Whispering Spruce Campground

Summer was hotter than usual for coastal Oregon, and the annual rains failed to arrive. It was, of course, perfect weather for vacationers, but the rangers were worried and talked of banning outdoor burning as had been done in several other western states that were experiencing one of the worst fire seasons in recent years. The grass turned yellow, the drooping goatsbeard, a pale beige, and the ferns were browning around the edges. The purple willow herb had already started to pod, the yellow broom dropped its flowers, and the salal berries took on their first fruity flush of color. A bumblebee flitted to a mass of milkweed, then buzzed over to another patch nearby, determined to get all the nectar they had to offer.

Dad had received complaints that the chipmunks were making pests of themselves and that nothing was safe from their greedy little mouths. He made a crude box trap, caught half a dozen, and carried them about a mile into the forest, but by the next day they were back. Joel threw one of them a walnut, which it snatched up and with lightning speed ripped off the outer layer with its teeth and ate the inside. Some of its friends arrived, and Joel decided to play a game with them. He tied a scrap of walnut meat to the end of a long string and tossed it in their direction. When one of them dived for it, Joel jerked it away out of reach. He tossed it to them several times, till one of them caught on and cut the string with its sharp teeth before Joel had time to pull it back. Then Joel tied a string between two small trees, and to it he tied two short strings that hung down, each with a piece of nut tied to the end. The chipmunks stared at the contraption for a few minutes. Finally one of them scampered along the horizontal string, but instead of climbing down the hanging string to get the nut, it pulled the nut up with its paws, chattering excitedly. Soon the rest of the chipmunks were doing the same.

"Smart little animals to figure that one out," Dad said as Joel tied two more pieces of walnut to the strings. This time the chipmunks entered into the fun of the game. They climbed into the tree, leaped at the nuts, and swung back and forth like little pendulums, their tails flying, until they had cut the string with their teeth. Then each fell to the ground with a piece of nut. Joel was delighted with the antics of his little friends, but Mom said that now they would never be rid of them and what should they tell the rest of the campers when they found out that the host was actually encouraging them!

Later in the day they drove to the estuary tidal flats to explore the nearby salt marsh. There was a drawbridge along the road to the salt marsh, and because it was up at the time, the traffic was backed up for almost a quarter of a mile. A tugboat was pulling a large crane up the river and experiencing difficulty getting it lined up to pass under the bridge. Finally the bridge operator decided he could no longer hold up the traffic, and he lowered the drawbridge so that Joel and his parents were able to continue their journey.

They turned off on a road that wound along a river until it reached the fertile salt marshes. Whistling swans nested in the marsh near the mouth of the river; and otter, beaver, mink, and raccoon abounded. The great blue heron lived there, along with wrens and crows and a host of wood ducks, myrtle warblers, and Pacific jumping mice.

They hiked the trail down to the marsh where the willow and alder thrust their roots deep into the water. Dad untangled a long length of discarded fishing line that had become wound around a clump of reeds.

"This stuff is dangerous to birds and other wildlife," he said. "They can easily get caught in it and have no way of extricating themselves. Every year many animals and birds die needlessly because of the carelessness of fishermen. I do wish they wouldn't leave fishing line lying about." He rolled the line into a ball and slipped it into his pocket.

They hiked farther along the trail till it reached a beach, then continued on down the beach till a river barred their way. They met two more hikers, an older couple, who stopped to talk about the beauty of forest and the ocean. Dad told them they were hosting at the national forest campground.

"That's a great way to spend the summer!" the man said.

His wife looked at Joel and smiled. "Sounds like you're having a wonderful time," she said. "It's the kind of thing my grandson would enjoy, I'm sure, except that he has got himself mixed up in religion. He actually told me the other day that he believes everything in the Bible is true. Can you imagine that?"

"I do too," Joel said quietly.

"You do!" she said, a little embarrassed. "Well, I hope I haven't offended you, but I honestly didn't realize people still felt that way. But we must hurry if we're to be home before dark," and with that they hastened on their way.

By then the air was beginning to turn chilly, and the tide had started running back into the ocean, making the river run more swiftly as it was being pulled out to the sea. A man in a wet suit hurried down the beach on the opposite side of the river and started to cross. He hesitated part way, appeared to change his mind, turned, and teetered on a stone for a moment. He tried to regain his footing but fell into the water. He shouted, then disappeared. The outrushing tide caught him and bore him rapidly out to sea. For a split second Joel and his parents stood rooted to the spot; then Joel broke into a run.

"There's a phone just down the road, near the dock," he said. "I saw it on our way over here. I'll call the police! Be back as soon as I can." Just minutes after Joel returned they heard the whap, whap, whap of a helicopter overhead skirting the coastline. A mile or two down the coast a motorboat roared out of its dock, flinging spray in its wake.

Joel and his parents stared out to sea watching for any sign of life, but they saw nothing.They clung to each other, shivering, not only because a chill wind blew along the shore but because of the helpless man somewhere out in the sea. The helicopter plied back and forth, across the mouth of the river. It finally fixed on a spot, where it stayed until the boat arrived, completed the rescue, and sped off toward the harbor.

"Thank God!" Mom exclaimed quietly. "Let's hope he'll be all right now." And now we'd better head back to the car, or we'll be caught out here in the dark. A small brown bat winged its way noiselessly through the air. It had no time to waste, for before evening was over it would have to eat almost a quarter of its weight in insects. A striped skunk crept out of its burrow to hunt for rodents, birds and bird eggs, reptiles, and insects. A shrew walked around tapping with its snout, looking for insects and worms. It too had no time to spare, for it had to feed almost continuously in order to stay alive, consuming food at the rate of three fourths of its own weight each hour! Under cover of darkness the marsh and the forest came alive with creatures in their search for food. Nothing was given to them. They had to hunt for it themselves.

The following day a man from the Coast Guard came by to report on the man they had plucked from the ocean.

"We got to him in the nick of time," he said. "The helicopter was just heading back to its station when your call came in; otherwise there's no telling how long it would have taken. The poor man was more dead than alive when we caught sight of him in the searchlight and hauled him into the boat. He must have been in shock because he told us to leave him alone, that he wanted to stay in the water. He must have been out of his mind to try to cross the river. He spent the night in the hospital, but they discharged him this morning. Don't be surprised if he gets in touch with you soon. I gave him your address."

But he never did. Joel remembered the story of the ten lepers Jesus healed, only one of whom returned to thank Him.

That afternoon an attractive young woman came to the door of the trailer and introduced herself. "We've rented the group camp area for the next four days," she said. "There'll be about twenty of us. I'm sort of the advance party. The rest will be coming later in the day."

"Yes, we knew you were arriving," Dad said. "The group camp area is all ready for you. There's a good supply of wood for you, and if there's anything else you need, let me know and I'll see what I can do to help."

She left but returned a short time later. "It's a super place," she began, "but I came to ask if you'd help me with my tent. I've never had one before and just can't get the hang of setting it up. My dad suggested I set it up in the yard before coming here, but you know how it is. I just didn't get around to it."

"I don't know much about tents," Dad said, "but I'll see what I can do." He went with her to the group area at the far end of the campground.

"When all else fails, read the instructions," he chuckled when he returned home. "We struggled with that tent for ages, till I finally asked if there were any instructions. She showed me a leaflet they'd given her in the shop. I checked the number of poles, and it was obvious that at least one was missing. That's why we couldn't get the thing to sit up straight. I rigged it with a broom handle, so it should hold until she leaves here. Then she can take it back to the store."

The rest of the group arrived later in the afternoon. They checked in with Dad, who explained the park rules. They asked if it would be all right to build a campfire that evening.

"Nice bunch of kids," Dad said. "I hope they enjoy their stay here. Apparently it's the first time most of them have camped in a forest." When he and Joel made their evening check of the campground the young people were sitting around a campfire talking and roasting marshmallows. They waved and called out "Goodnight!" when Joel and Dad passed by.

Just after midnight, there was a knock at the trailer door. Dad roused himself from sleep, slipped into a bathrobe, and went to investigate. "What is it?" he asked sleepily, trying not to sound annoyed.

"You've got to stop them," the visitor said heatedly. "They've been yelling and singing for over an hour and playing their music so loud I can't sleep. I spoke to them about it, but they only laughed in my face."

"Stop who?" Dad asked, still not fully awake.

"The kids in the group area," the man said. "Listen. You can hear them from here, and where I am it's enough to make your ears hemorrhage."

"Hold on and I'll be right over," Dad said, pulling on his boots. "They're good kids, and I'm sure I'll be able to quiet them down. Sorry you've been disturbed." His visitor went off muttering.

As he got closer to the group area, the noise became louder and louder. He heard shouting, laughing, and above it all a radio blaring out the latest pop music. Two young people were rocking about dreamily in each other's arms. Three or four more were chasing each other in and out of the restrooms, throwing water, screaming hysterically all the while. Others sprawled around the fire drinking beer and laughing uproariously.

"Hold it!" Dad yelled above the din. "Turn that thing off!" He pointed to the radio, but no one paid the slightest attention to him. He spoke directly to a young man by the fire, but all he got was an impudent grin.

"We ain't hurting anyone," one of them said. "Go back to bed and get some sleep."

"The rest of the campers can't sleep because of the noise you're making," Dad said. "The rule is no noise after ten o'clock, and it's after midnight. If you can't be quiet I'll have to call the sheriff."

"Listen guys," one of them said lazily. "He's threatening us. Can you believe it? Says he's going to call the sheriff." Then turning to Dad he said, "We paid for this place. We're here to have fun, and neither you nor anyone else can stop us, so beat it."

"We'll see about that," Dad said quietly. "I'm telling you for the last time, either you quiet down or you'll have to leave."

The young man sat up quickly. "OK, guys, you heard the man. Cool it or we'll have the sheriff up here."

His words seemed to take effect. The group quieted down immediately, turned off the radio, and everyone went back to their tents. After he'd made sure the party was over, Dad trudged wearily home to resume his interrupted sleep.

The next knock came about two thirty. It was the same man who had complained earlier. "They're at it again," he said angrily. "Listen! We've got to get some sleep, and they're driving us crazy with their noise. Can't you do something?"

"Enough's enough," Dad said grimly, reaching for the telephone. A few minutes later the sheriff arrived. Dad stepped outside to talk to him.

"These college kids are all the same," he said "Think they can't have any fun unless they tear the place apart. I'll put a stop to it if I have to lock the whole lot of them up for the night. Go back to bed; I'll take care of them." He drove off to the group camp area, the red light atop his car flashing ominously.

It was a long time before Dad could go back to sleep, and he wasn't in the best mood the following morning. "At least I wasn't disturbed again after the sheriff spoke to them," he said, "so he must have got them to listen. What a pity they made nuisances of themselves and kept the entire campground awake."

Soon after breakfast the ranger stopped by to say he'd been over to talk to the young people and told them they had to be out of the campground before lunchtime. "Of course they were all sound asleep," he said, "and mighty upset when I woke them up. One of them actually asked me what a person had to do to get some peace and quiet around here! Give them time to get their belongings together. After they've gone, you'd better police the area. They're bound to leave a mess."

Dad promised to take care of it.

The young people had already taken down their tents and were stashing their belongings in their vehicles when he and Joel went over to the group area later that morning. "Here's your broom," said the girl whose tent he had helped set up the day before. She looked at the ground. "Guess you heard we have to leave. Sorry we got you out of bed last night, but I honestly didn't think we were that loud."

"I'm sorry too," Dad said. "Sorry it had to end this way."

When the last car had pulled out Joel took a large garbage bag and began collecting the empty cans and bottles, the rolls of soggy toilet paper, and other rubbish. Dad discovered that they had mutilated several young trees, spray-painted the women's restroom, broken one of the sinks, and smashed the hand dryer with a tire iron.

"A pity," Dad remarked. "Animals have lived in these forests for generations without causing pollution or destruction, but in a short time people can turn a beautiful spot into a rubbish heap." He asked Joel if he had read the Bible verse with God's instructions to the children of Israel when they were about to enter the Promised Land. "It says, 'God walketh in the midst of thy camp, to deliver thee . . . ; therefore shall thy camp be holy: that he see no unclean thing in thee, and turn away from thee. [Deuteronomy 23:14].' God expects us to keep our surroundings clean," Dad said. "It's an insult to Him when we spoil His lovely creation with garbage."

"It's like going into someone's beautiful garden and throwing litter around," Joel said.

Later the ranger said that he had written a letter to the college requesting them to post a notice on the bulletin board that students would no longer be welcome to use the group camping area. "Not only that, but it will be closed until we can make the repairs," he added grimly.

"What a pity that a few thoughtless kids have spoiled it for everybody else in that school," Mom said.

"And for themselves as well," the ranger added, "because not only did they cut their vacation short and lose the fee they paid, but they'll be billed for damages too."

Dad and Joel scrubbed the vandalized restroom, and one of the rangers repainted it; but it was a long time before another sink was installed, and the hand dryer never was replaced. That night it rained, washing away the last traces of the mess in the group camping area.

"Perhaps the rain was nature's way of cleansing the ugly memories of the night before," Joel said.

Chapter 9
Deer Mouse Finds a New Home

A large-eared, white-footed mouse, or deer mouse as he is sometimes called, was born in a comfortable overstuffed chair in the attic of a big house. As he grew up, this particular mouse became intimately acquainted with every room in the house. Sometimes he sat quietly under the long sitting-room curtains while Mrs. Fisk played the piano, and once he crept into her bedroom while she was asleep and actually scampered across the foot of her bed! His favorite room was the kitchen. Its cupboards abounded with all sorts of good things to eat such as flour and cereal, nuts, and dried fruit; and he spent as much time there as possible. It was a dangerous place, though. Once his five brothers and two sisters went off on a hunting expedition and didn't return. But right now these troubling thoughts never entered his head, for he was on his way to enjoy a breakfast of cornflakes.

He smelled the cheese before he saw it. He turned a corner in the cupboard and there it was: the ripest, yellowest hunk of cheese he'd ever dreamed of. His whiskers twitched in anticipation. He crept up close and snatched at the cheese, and instantly he heard a tremendous crack. The snare of a steel trap snapped down on the wood and flung him into the air. He landed with a thud on his back.

His tiny heart palpitating wildly, the mouse fled back through the hole in the corner of the cupboard, across the kitchen floor, and through an open door. He blinked in the sunshine outside. Up to now he'd only known the inside, and he felt afraid. The bright sunshine made his head hurt, and he wanted desperately to hide. He scampered across the garden path, ran up the wheels of a vehicle standing nearby, and sneaked through a tiny doorway. The opening inside was filled with warm, dark insulation. When his nerves had quieted he crept out of the insulation and squeezed behind a drawer. He crawled over a pile of blankets and out into a small bedroom. He didn't know it, but he was in Mrs. Fisk's camper.

He found a few crumbs on the kitchen floor, but that was all. A careful inspection of the cupboards revealed nothing, so hungry and still shaken by his ordeal, he crept back into the insulation and fell asleep.

When he awoke he tried to leave through the tiny door, but now it was shut tight. He spent all that night tearing off bits of insulation, searching for wood shavings, and pulling loose threads and pieces of fluff from the blankets, until he had formed a nest in one of the walls of the camper. This new nest was every bit as comfortable as his old one in the overstuffed chair.

Then he made a tour of the camper. What fun he had scampering up and down! He investigated every nook and cranny, and joy of joys, he discovered half a dozen peanuts in a cellophane bag that had fallen behind the sofa many months before. By the time the first morning light peeped in the camper windows he was very tired, so he returned to his nest in the insulation.

He awoke terrified. His home had begun to shake and rattle alarmingly, and it was with difficulty that he managed to cling to the insulation for support. Hour after hour the nightmare continued. Just as he was wondering how much longer he could retain his tenuous hold, the shaking and rattling stopped.

Soon he heard footsteps, the familiar rattling of pots and pans, and in no time tantalizing smells reached his nose: fresh bread, vegetable soup, milk, and warm brownies. Suddenly he realized that he was very, very hungry.

At last the sounds of the kitchen ceased, and everything was quiet in the camper, so the tiny mouse ventured out of his hiding place, and now it was his turn to eat! He saw brownies on a plate by the kitchen sink, and he nibbled a corner off one of them. Mmmm. It was delicious. Next he turned his attention to the garbage can, and here was a feast indeed: juicy potato peelings, a delicate morsel of bread, and a tiny sliver of apple. He crouched on the floor, holding each bit of food in his tiny paws, and ate with relish. His hunger finally appeased, he began to race up and down the camper, poking his pointed little face into every corner. The smell of cheese drew him to one of the cupboards, and he started to gnaw his way through the wood. He didn't have to worry about wearing down his teeth. They would grow back out as fast as he wore them down. At daybreak he retreated to his nest. Before falling asleep he decided that life here would be every bit as good as it had been in his old place.

Mrs. Fisk was outside her camper sitting in the sun when Dad and Joel walked by the following morning on their regular tour of the campground.

"Good morning!" Dad called to her. "Beautiful morning isn't it?"

"Gorgeous," she said.

"How long will you be visiting?" Dad asked.

"A week, I hope," she said. "It depends on the

weather. But I have a little problem and need some advice."

"What is it?" Dad asked.

"It's silly," she said. "but there's a mouse in my camper. It kept me awake all night long, scampering up and down and rustling the paper in the garbage can. How can I get rid of it? I'm terrified that it may gnaw on the electrical wiring. And horror of horrors, what if it has babies! Then what will I do?"

"How about getting a cat?" Joel suggested.

"Most cats are much too lazy to catch mice," she said. "And besides, I don't really care for cats or they for me."

"How do you suppose the mouse got in?" Dad asked.

"I've no idea," Mrs. Fisk said, "except I have them in my house in Portland. I set out traps and caught several, but traps won't do in a camper. I'd be sure to catch my toe in one of them."

"Did you leave the camper open back in Portland?" Dad asked.

"No, except the little door to the storage area. I had that open for a couple of days to dry out. Do you think it could have got in that way?"

"Quite possibly," Dad told her. "Why don't you leave it open again for a little while? Perhaps it'll leave by the same way it came in. It's worth trying."

"Or bring others in with it," Mrs. Fisk said gloomily.

"If that doesn't work," Dad said, continuing his walk, "we'll have to come up with another idea. Let me know what happens, won't you?"

When white-footed mouse woke up later in the day, he felt warm sunshine flooding his nest. Looking about he discovered that the little door was open again. He peered outside. Straight ahead were trees as far as he could see, and under them were seeds and scented berries bursting with juice. He decided to explore this wonderful new world where there was food for the gathering, and bring back some of it to store in his nest. He scampered about the forest floor, rousting tiny insects from their hiding places, retrieving succulent seeds and nuts from under leaves, and sampling the ripe berries. At last he decided to return home, but when he got there the tiny door was closed. He was locked out! There was nothing to do but go back to the sweet-smelling forest. He hunted around till he found an empty nest in a pile of brush. It would have to do, he decided, until he had made other plans for his bold new adventure into the world beyond four walls.

Several days later, far away from the forest, he found a snug castle in a corncrib where he met a lady mouse. Together they raised a family that knew nothing of walls and cheese and steel spring traps.

"Did our plan work?" Dad asked Mrs. Fisk when they met the following day.

"Oh, yes," she said smiling happily. "Thanks to your advice, I had a peaceful night. Now I can enjoy my camper again."

Dad told Joel later that he had regretted suggesting she leave the storage door open. "I had visions of a whole army of mice taking up residence in the camper," he said, "and I'd have been to blame. I'm glad that everything turned out all right."

Because of the continued warm weather, the berries ripened sooner than usual on the Oregon coast. One morning Mom armed herself with a big basin and cotton gloves and set out to comb the campground for the ripest and juiciest berries she could find. The salal berries were the first to be ready for picking, so she gathered enough to make an experimental salal pie.

"What does *salal* mean?" Joel asked at noon when Mom set a piece of pie in front of him for dessert.

"It's an Indian name for a shrub that was used extensively by the coastal Indians many years ago," Mom said. "They thought very highly of its black, aromatic fruits."

"When an explorer named David Douglas arrived in Oregon," Dad said, "he liked the salal so much that he sent samples of it to England and Europe, hoping to promote it as a berry plant. But even though it has become useful there as a dense ground cover, it never caught on as an edible fruit."

The pie had an unusual woodsy taste, and Dad said he'd rather Mom left the salal berries for the birds and mammals to enjoy. So from then on, she picked berries of the raspberry family—salmonberries and blackcaps, whose ripe fruit comes clean of the core. Those whose fruit doesn't separate from the core are of the blackberry family. Later she picked huge quantities of shiny black huckleberries for pancakes and pies and also for jellies and jams. She set aside several small jars of this late summer treat, attractively labeled and fragrant with the scents of an Oregon summer, as gifts for friends and acquaintances at Christmastime.

On one of her berrying expeditions Mom heard screams coming from a clump of blackberry bushes. She hurried over to see what could be the matter. A little girl was sobbing and jumping up and down wildly. Her two brothers were laughing at her, calling her a baby, and telling her to stop crying. "Big girls don't cry like that," they said.

Mom took the little girl in her arms. "What's the matter, sweetheart?" she asked.

"A bee stung me on my arm," she sobbed. "It hurts."

"I know it does," Mom said, and the sobbing stopped for a moment.

"The stinger is still in it," Mom said after examining the child's arm. "We've got to get it out." She gently scraped out the poisonous barb with her fingernail, explaining that pulling it out would only squeeze the rest of the pain-producing venom into the little girl's skin.

"Did you know that when a bee stings you it dies?" Mom asked. She explained that the stinger is attached to the bee's inside and comes away when it stings someone. "Only girl bees can sting," she said, "and in colonies of bees, wasps, and ants, most are girls." She paused and wiped the tears from the little girl's eyes. "Now let's go to the trailer, and I'll put something on your arm to make it feel better," she said.

Back at home Mom washed the little girl's arm and coated it with a soothing ointment. "I was stung once when I was a little girl," Mom told her. "I still remember how much it hurt. They could hear me screaming for miles. Even now I'm afraid of bees."

"I hate them," said the little girl. "I wish there weren't any bees."

"Without bees to pollinate the flowers there would be no fruit," Mom said. "Although it hurts if one of them stings us, we need bees to work for us. And just think what the world would be like without the honey they make!" The little girl laughed and in a very short time had forgotten her painful experience.

Chapter 10
Mr. Friendly's Sand Castle

When Mr. Friendly pulled into the campground, he announced that he had come for the annual Labor Day Sand Sculpting Competition sponsored by local businessmen.

"Sand sculpting, what's that?" Joel asked.

"It's a very ancient art," Mr. Friendly explained. "It's almost as old as sand itself, I expect. It's a way for people to express themselves in sand, temporarily, of course." Mr. Friendly explained that he competed in sand sculpting all up and down the West Coast, from Santa Barbara in California to Cannon Beach in Oregon. "Come down to the beach next Sunday and see for yourself," he said to Joel. "You're in for a treat, I can assure you."

Joel's parents said they would be busy at the campground that day, but they wanted him to go to the beach with Mr. Friendly and learn about sand sculpting. "Perhaps next year you'll be able to enter the competition too," Dad said with a chuckle.

There was a carnival air at the beach when Joel and Mr. Friendly arrived just after dawn the next Sunday morning. Several people had already staked out places on the sandy beach where they could create their sand sculpting entries. Mr. Friendly explained that the best place to build was at the tide line—the point the tide reaches at its very highest. It is marked by a wavy line of foam dotted with seaweed. "Where the sand is firm and more compact is the best place to build," he said.

There were four classes of competition: ages six to twelve, thirteen to eighteen, nineteen and over, and groups of three or more people over thirteen.

"Sand sculpting is judged on the basis of originality, workmanship, and composition," Mr. Friendly said. He staked out a smooth, flat section of beach and set up his tools beside him: a shovel, bucket, and paper cups for molds. The judges were waiting in flag-covered dune buggies." "When they sound a bell, the beach will become alive with activity," he said.

"What are you going to make?" Joel asked. Mr. Friendly said that he planned to build a castle. "I've been building castles for years," he said. "This one will be Mont-Saint-Michel, a Gothic castle on the Normandy coast of France. It's over a thousand years old. This famous castle is an offshore island at high tide, but becomes part of the mainland at low tide. Over the centuries a host of invaders sought to take the castle by force, but drowned in the onrushing tides. Today, of course," he said, "a long causeway connects the island with the mainland."

The bell sounded, and Mr. Friendly began piling up the damp sand with lightning speed. "The wetter the sand, the longer the castle will last," he explained. He built a series of square, squat buildings, leaning buildings, buildings with spires and windows, turrets, and battlements from where, centuries earlier, archers shot at those who were unwise enough to try to storm Mont-Saint-Michel. He built round towers, hexagonal towers, and towers connected by intricate little pathways. His castle grew and grew till it looked like a giant iced cake.

He talked as he worked, his hands keeping pace with his tongue. He told Joel about the famous castles on the Rhine River in Germany. "The Marksburg Castle was built centuries ago by a lawless robber family who preyed on the boats that sailed along the river at its base." he said. "Sad to say, under the Markus Tower, named for the beloved writer of the Gospel of Mark, was one of the most gruesome and fearful torture chambers in all of Europe."

Joel shuddered. "Poor Mark," he said. "He would sure be sorry if he knew his name was given to such a terrible place."

"Another castle you might be interested in," Mr. Friendly continued, patting down the sand of another tower, "is Karlštejn's Castle near Prague, Czechoslovakia. That's where the followers of Jan Huss, one of the forerunners of the Reformation, took refuge when the church courts condemned him to die for his beliefs— beliefs that we still hold dear today."

He told Joel other stories of famous castles such as the Windsor Castle in England, the Kremlin in Russia, and Heidelberg Castle in Germany, all with cruel histories of violence and bloodshed.

Joel wandered down the beach to admire other samples of sand sculpting, here a ferocious lion crouched on the sand gazing out to sea, there a crocodile with a backbone of shells that almost appeared to crawl along the beach. One person was building a windmill, another a big clock that told the time with hands of sand and figures of shells. Even the children were sand sculpting, making castles with moats that refused to hold water, sand boats with driftwood paddles, and funny faces grinning at the absurdity of it all.

Joel went back to see how Mr. Friendly's castle was progressing and found it almost finished. The tide had turned and was already beginning to creep up the beach, wave by wave, intent on destroying all their imaginative labors.

Dad and Mom arrived and walked up and down the beach in astonishment. A miniature city of castles and towers had sprung up, populated with fierce animals and monsters.

A bell sounded and the participants wearily laid aside their tools. They sat down on the sand beside their masterpieces and waited hopefully, while the judges drove by slowly in their dune buggies. Some contestants groaned aloud. "I didn't have the time to finish," said one. "If only I had had ten more minutes," said another. Everyone straightened his back and flexed his legs while the judges scribbled on their score pads. Joel and his parents sat on the sand beside Mr. Friendly, watching the relentless tide advancing slowly up the beach.

"Reminds me of old King Canute," Mr. Friendly said. "Ever heard of him, Joel?"

Joel said he hadn't.

"He was a Danish king who ruled over England many years ago," Mr. Friendly said. "He was a good and wise king, well loved by those of his court. People began to say that he was so great he was like a god." King Canute didn't let such foolish talk go to his head. Instead, he decided to teach them a lesson. He ordered them to bring his throne down to the beach and set it at the edge of the ocean."

Mr. Friendly paused, then told how the king sat on his throne and ordered all his servants and advisers to stand beside him. "With his entire court watching, he ordered the tide to stop. It continued advancing, and soon King Canute and his court were up to their necks in water. They had been made to look foolish, since no man on earth can stop the incoming tide."

By now the judges had completed the entire circuit

and returned to announce the names of the winners in each category. Mr. Friendly didn't receive a prize, but he said he didn't mind. "The pleasure is in the making of the castle," he said. "There will be other sand sculpting contests on other beaches."

The sun was nearing the western horizon. Many of the contestants went home, but others stayed to watch the inrushing tide attack their works of art, nibbling at a corner here, washing down a wall there, toppling a tower, or wiping the smile off a monster's face. Mr. Friendly's castle lost its strong outer wall first; then one by one its lower towers crumbled. The sun sank lower and lower. It became half an orange, then a quarter, and then it disappeared beyond the ocean. The sky blazed briefly, then began to darken. Bonfires sprang up all along the shore as people waited for the final destruction of their sandy masterpieces.

The last days of summer were ending as surely as the sand castles were crumbling. Tomorrow would be the end of the camping season. Whispering Spruce Campground would be closed until the following year. In the forest the jumping mice were getting fat in readiness for their winter hibernation. Chipmunks and squirrels had already begun filling their secret storehouses with nuts, and the black-tailed deer were retreating deeper into the trees. Some were already in process of changing their summer coats for winter ones—brown tinged with grey or red. The warblers were heading south to California and Mexico, while hosts of sparrows and other birds that had spent the summer in Canada had begun to take up their residence in Whispering Spruce Campground.

The next morning Joel and his parents left the campground, and some time later the gate was swung across the entrance and locked until the following spring.

Joel knew that the winter rains would wash away the dirt and grime left by people, and the forest would revert once more to its original inhabitants.